good
PARENTS
tough
TIMES

Charlene C. Giannetti & Margaret Sagarese

good
PARENTS
tough
TIMES

how your catholic faith

provides hope and guidance

in times of crisis

LOYOLAPRESS.

CHICAGO

LOYOLAPRESS.

3441 N. ASHLAND AVENUE
CHICAGO, ILLINOIS 60657
(800) 621-1008
WWW.LOYOLABOOKS.ORG

A previous edition of this book titled *The Patience of a Saint: How Faith Can Sustain You During Tough Times in Parenting* was published in 2002 by Broadway Books in paperback (ISBN 0-7679-0901-1) and by Doubleday Books in hardcover (ISBN 0-385-50038-6).

Scripture quotations are taken from the New Jerusalem Bible, copyright © 1985 by Darton, Longman & Todd, Ltd. and Doubleday, a division of Random House, Inc.

The English translation of the *Salve, Regina* (Hail Holy Queen, pages 224–25) from *A Book of Prayers* © 1982, International Committee on English in the Liturgy, Inc. All rights reserved.

English translation of the Sign of the Cross, the Apostles' Creed, Our Father, Glory Be to the Father, and Hail Mary (pages 223–24) by the International Consultation on English Texts.

Cover and interior design by Tracey Harris Sainz

Library of Congress Cataloging-in-Publication Data

Giannetti, Charlene C.

Good parents, tough times : how your Catholic faith provides hope and guidance in times of crisis / Charlene C. Giannetti and Margaret Sagarese.

p. cm.

Includes bibliographical references.

ISBN 0-8294-2073-8

1. Parenting—Religious aspects—Catholic Church. 2. Christian saints. I. Sagarese, Margaret. II. Title.

BX2352.G53 2004

248.4'82—dc22

2004014657

Printed in the United States of America

05 06 07 08 09 10 11 Bang 10 9 8 7 6 5 4 3 2 1

To my sister, Lorraine,
the saint in my life.—C.C.G.

In memory of my mother, Grace,
who had the soul of a saint.—M.S.

Contents

Introduction

I made a major mistake this weekend. My fourteen-year-old daughter took me to my limit. I slapped her. I pray God will give me the strength and knowledge to deal with her.

My daughter was caught shoplifting. Every day I wake up scared to death of what she will do next. I am losing my health over this. What can I do?

I have a fourteen-year-old son who is out of control. I find myself saying as a mantra, "I love him, I love him," just to remind myself that I do during the worst times.

These sentiments and others like them come from parents whose struggles with their adolescents have taken over their lives and reduced them to despair. We have often heard such laments from parents who come to our talks or visit us online at www.parentsoup.com. Many of these parents are in shock. They don't know what has happened to their child, and they worry that they have lost him or her forever.

These are tough times to parent an adolescent. School shootings, substance abuse, sexual harassment, AIDS, eating disorders, violence, depression—all are part and parcel of our children's world. The messages our children receive from the media contradict the values we try desperately to teach them.

At the same time, we are with them less. With more dual working couples and an increasing number of single-parent homes, our children often spend time after school home alone and are more vulnerable to outside influences.

We know from our experience as parenting experts that the issues that crop up during adolescence are complex and resist easy solutions. Sometimes parents reach a point with a troubled adolescent when it seems that change is hopeless. We've tried everything humanly possible, and we are frustrated by our lack of progress. At this point, we need to look to a higher source for help and inspiration.

In this book, we will look to the saints, ordinary men and women who faced challenges, tragedies, and violence with incredible courage and fortitude. Their lives were filled with miracles and mystery. The heart-wrenching tales we recount within these pages can inspire and encourage all of us to build our spiritual character, develop coping mechanisms, and multiply our religious resources.

We hope that whether you are a mother, father, stepparent, or grandparent, you will keep this book close at hand. The drama will entice you to turn the pages, while the stories themselves will bring home the truth that all things are possible with God, even rescuing your out-of-control child.

THE TRIALS OF PARENTING

How do you parent a struggling child? It helps to be up-to-date on the latest parenting techniques. But even the most well-intentioned parent armed with this information needs more. A parent needs faith, love, hope, and the patience of a saint.

We came to this understanding the hard way, through our own parenting conflicts. How ironic, we thought: here we are, the experts, advising other parents, and we are unable to cope ourselves. We did everything humanly possible, following our own dictums, yet when all was said and done, we felt helpless. We worried about our children becoming depressed, falling in with unsavory friends, or possibly resorting to substance abuse.

As we worried about our own children, we listened to other parents who felt powerless. One mother asked: "Why should parenting involve so much suffering?"

Her comment brought to mind the Virgin Mother. She gave birth in a stable. Her child ran off to the temple, and she panicked until she found him. Jesus took on a lifestyle that was, to say the least, unconventional. He opened himself up to ridicule. Mary watched him be dragged through the streets and die on the cross. Where was the joy in her parenting?

Considering Mary's struggles led us to explore the lives of other saints. Learning about them had been a big part of our religious education, and we saw that they might be able to offer the help we had been looking for. Many saints did not lead saintly lives in the beginning. These individuals are accessible to us, and their lives and words offer much inspiration.

Some saints stand out because of their own experiences and how they coped. St. Monica's son Augustine acted out during adolescence and resisted Catholicism. For thirty long years Monica prayed for his conversion. It finally happened, and he went on to become a saint himself, an encouraging outcome for all mothers with headstrong sons.

Many saints lived in biblical times, but their lives and experiences parallel our lives and many of the situations facing our children. With her prayers, St. Rita managed to turn around her abusive husband and two difficult sons before they died. Dealing with an out-of-control child often places great stress on a marriage. How many couples could find comfort in St. Rita's example?

St. Agnes was only thirteen when she was martyred. A beautiful girl, she was aggressively pursued by many suitors, but she chose to remain a virgin. Could we pray to her that our daughters will find the strength to use good judgment in their youthful relationships? What about St. Jude, the patron saint of hopeless causes? What could seem more hopeless than attempting to parent an angry, defiant adolescent?

Then there is St. Joseph. Imagine the faith necessary for him to marry a pregnant woman and accept her destiny as the mother of God. He was hardworking, honest, and humble. How many fathers could learn from him?

Consider Mary's own parents, St. Anne and St. Joachim. Their daughter's unplanned pregnancy threatened their happiness, but they faced this trial with great faith and courage. Could parents whose daughters face unplanned pregnancies draw solace and strength from the examples set by these two great saints?

All these saints took a leap of faith, and from them we learn that sometimes it is the only thing that can take a parent from the despair of today to the hope of tomorrow. After we have done everything humanly possible, all we can do is continue to trust in God. And to help us strengthen our faith and belief, we can turn to the saints, ordinary men and women who also struggled with everyday concerns and managed to rise above them. Their examples can inspire us, comfort us, bring us closer to God, and, ultimately, help us restore our relationships with our children.

The Power of Prayer

The old saying "God helps those who help themselves" still resonates. Praying for a troubled adolescent is a way of helping, although of course prayer is not always enough on its own. If a parent suspects that a child is using drugs, for example, the adolescent may need counseling or perhaps even something more serious, such as a rehabilitation or wilderness therapy program. Along the way, however, prayer can occupy the mind and spirit and create a sea of calm in the middle of a storm. It can be a refuge when all else has failed.

Prayer is not a passive activity. A parent can pray and feel as if she is doing something. The routine of prayer, the rituals involved—saying novenas or rosaries, lighting candles, attending Mass—provide an activity and a focus. Concentrating on the saints makes the exercise more personal. It's like taking a journey with a friend. The saints travel with us in spirit to offer support and understanding. Their lives, too, were once filled with turmoil. They can empathize. We know they are listening.

This book is organized into eight chapters, each focused on a specific virtue: charity, knowledge, faith, hope, patience, serenity, truth, humility. Within each chapter we will draw from real-life experiences of parents we have met at our talks and online, and we will draw parallels between these crises and those endured by the saints.

We will guide you on reestablishing a connection with the saints through various activities—praying novenas, reading the Bible, reciting the rosary, and making pilgrimages, to name a few. We have also provided discussion questions at the end of each chapter that you can use on your own or in a small group, depending on your preference. Some questions are more appropriate for personal reflection, while others lend themselves more to group discussion. Choose whichever questions fit you best. These exercises are simple yet will produce profound results.

We live in modern times, but the problems parents face today echo those confronted by the saints. Their lives still have relevance. The Bible says, "There is a season for everything, a time for every occupation under the heaven." These are tough times to parent—and times to look to heaven, to the saints, for inspiration.

chapter one

Charity

[Love] is always ready to make allowances, to
trust, to hope and to endure whatever comes.

—ST. PAUL, 1 CORINTHIANS 13:7

L oving our children during adolescence can become a soul-searching struggle. How do you love a chronically angry, stubborn teenager? How can you respect a slothful, cruel, or promiscuous adolescent who shows no inkling of your values? When you are on the receiving end of continual hostility, and even verbal abuse, how do you respond with kindness?

And yet a child cannot survive, much less flourish, without the love and support of adults. Unconditional love is the birthright of every child. A parent is supposed to love a child. All parents fully intend to love a child—forever and always.

Then adolescence happens. Some children are bent on behaving in ways that mothers and fathers and stepparents find repugnant. Many such parents find themselves thinking the unthinkable: *I don't like my child anymore.* And they harbor a secret shame because their hearts have become so cold toward one of their own. Many have come to us with such unchari-table confessions. One mother pleaded:

Help! I don't like my daughter! My eleven-year-old daugh-
ter is full of anger. She tried to strangle a classmate because

the girl "pissed her off." I have not admitted this—even to the counselor we've been seeing—but I am having very negative feelings toward my daughter. She is my child, but I can't stand to be around her. And I am embarrassed by her. She has a bad attitude from the moment she gets up in the morning till she goes to bed at night. She has alienated herself from all the girls in her class, from her siblings, her stepfather, and everyone with whom she comes into contact. She is very good at hurting everyone around her. I wish I could say this behavior is new for her, but it's not. She has been this way since she was a little girl. It's just getting worse. My husband and I have come to the conclusion that this is the way she is, and we will just have to deal with her the best we can. I am scared for her, for myself, and for our family.

Running out of love as a mother, father, stepparent, or caregiver is a double-edged sword. You have to deal with emotional bankruptcy and the self-inflicted judgment of being inadequate. A parent's love and ability to nurture aren't supposed to run dry. When they do, guilt rushes in to fill the empty space.

This love drought happens at the worst possible moment. The fact is that when your child is at his or her worst, that is when your love is needed the *most*.

Perhaps the image of Christ turning the other cheek to derision comes to mind. Yet when your child hurts you deeply, it's not always possible to be so Christlike. It's hard to emulate Jesus' gesture because your own child isn't supposed to be your nemesis.

In this chapter we will show you how to reconnect with love. We will deliver a number of transforming lessons and introduce you to the saints who can show you how to live those lessons. To help you keep love uppermost in your mind and in your actions, we are going to send you on a scavenger hunt for concrete tokens that you can hold on to when you need to love more and love better. We will help you find ways to renew your capacity for warmth, understanding, forgiveness, and affection when you are faced with rebellion, defiance, and even hatred.

GOD THE CELESTIAL ALCHEMIST

In medieval times a mysterious science called alchemy surfaced. Alchemists holed up in castle laboratories, stewing over cauldrons and beakers, trying to master the transmutation of base metals into gold. Alas, the alchemists never quite succeeded at materializing those King Midas fantasies. It turned out that there was no scientific way to change common worthless metals into gold. There is, however, one alchemist who can transform anything common into something of value: God. He is a celestial alchemist because he can transform us with his love. If we turn to God, even in our meanest or our most hard-hearted state, he can overhaul our hearts by infusing us with his everlasting love. When you are hate filled and feeling loveless, realize that transformation is within reach.

TRANSFORM VENGEANCE
INTO FORGIVENESS

A teenager pushes you over the edge. You rave inappropriately and say things you wish you could take back. You feel disgusted with yourself after a screaming match. This behavior becomes a pattern. You don't like the person your child has become. And even worse, you don't like the person you have become.

One way to rediscover love is to embrace forgiveness. The first step toward forgiveness—and toward finding your way back to being that loving parent you so want to be—is learning to forgive yourself. You are, after all, only human. Even though you are the adult and your son or daughter is the child, you are still a person who needs love. When your teenager withholds love and delivers only anger and pain over time, it's natural for you to lash out or silently turn away and harden your heart.

Be honest with yourself. Acknowledge your diminished capacity to love this child. Only then can you forgive yourself and commit to trying harder.

The next step is to forgive your child. You have every right to be angry at a misbehaving teenager. A teen who dumps on you, your spouse, and his siblings is betraying you and sabotaging the family. Yet you must learn to separate the hurtful behavior from the child. You had no trouble making that distinction when your son was five or six. You would say, "I love you, Jake, but I don't like the way you hit your baby brother." Now, it's harder to make distinctions between who he is and how he acts. His behaviors—disrespectful talk, lack of consideration, brooding tantrums—pollute nearly every family interaction.

Stepparents can have an even harder struggle with forgiveness. A stepparent "inherits" a child after committing to a new spouse. This communion creates an unnatural family unit, a family of strangers. Love doesn't naturally bloom between the stepparent and stepchild in the same way it does for the re-marrying adults. Stepchildren want their old families back, not the newfangled hybrid.

Stepmothers who are raising stepchildren teeter in positions of authority, often without having the support of the biological mother or the goodwill of the child. Many of these women find themselves raising an exiled teenager, meaning one whom Mom couldn't handle any longer and shipped off to live with Dad and the new stepmom. Stepfathers are in many cases the head of a blended household and receive little gratitude—much less love—for their contributions of time, energy, and money.

Raising a troubled teen is hard enough. Being responsible for someone else's troubled adolescent is a burden no one but those in the predicament can fully appreciate. So if you are in such a situation and resenting every minute with your stepchildren, forgive yourself for not being able to measure up to your fantasies of the kind of stepparent you think you should be. And forgive your stepchild. He is involuntarily stuck in the trauma of his parent's divorce. He is a hostage in a future he never wanted or planned for himself.

We know that converting resentment, even hatred, into forgiveness is easier said than done. Let God inspire you, as he is the perfect model. Think of how he forgives our sins, no matter how many, how mortal, or how frequent. All we need to do is ask his forgiveness, and he grants it. God's forgiving nature is mirrored in the lives of many saints. St. Maria Goretti is just one.

Maria was born in 1890, one of six children in a farm-working family who lived in Roman Campagna. Her father died of malaria when Maria was just six. Her mother became one of the original single working mothers. With no man to support her or her children, Mom took her husband's place in the fields. Maria stayed at home and took over the household duties and the raising of the younger children.

As Maria grew into early adolescence, she began to look older than her age. When she was twelve, she caught the eye of a neighbor, a twenty-one-year-old young man by the name of Alessandro Serenelli. He began stopping by when Maria's mother was working and flirting with the young girl. Maria was instantly uncomfortable. She discouraged his advances but was reluctant to tell her mother about them for fear of causing problems. To her way of thinking, her family had already seen enough hardship and catastrophe. Suppose she made trouble and her mother got fired?

One night, Alessandro visited and forced himself on Maria. When she attempted to fight him off, he stabbed her fourteen times with his knife. According to what we know of this incident, their final conversation went something like this:

Alessandro ordered, "Submit or die."

Maria replied, "Death, but not sin."

Before she died, Maria uttered her last words. They were strange and unexpected. She said that she wanted to be with him in paradise.

Alessandro left his victim bleeding. When her mother came home, she rushed Maria to the hospital. She clung to life for the next twenty-four hours, long enough to display concern for her family. *What would become of them without her help?* she worried. Furthermore, she prayed for the soul of Alessandro, forgave him, and hoped this incident wouldn't bring ruin on his family. Then Maria died.

In the aftermath of this cold-blooded crime, Alessandro expressed no remorse for murdering the young girl and was sentenced to thirty years in prison. During the eighth year of his incarceration, he had a vision of Maria. Dressed in white, she stood in a garden, carrying white lilies. She offered the flowers to Alessandro and smiled lovingly. He was stricken with regret and became totally devoted to the memory of Maria.

When released from prison, Alessandro begged Maria's mother for forgiveness. Eventually Alessandro became a Capuchin lay brother and told many of his vision and how it changed his heart. When Maria Goretti was canonized in 1950, her mother and her murderer both attended the ceremony.

St. Maria Goretti managed to hold on to love and exude forgiveness even as her own life ebbed under the knife of a murderer. If she could forgive the loss of her life and the man who cut that life short, she can help us find forgiveness for the crimes and shortcomings we experience in our life and within our family.

Take cues from Maria. She didn't spend hours telling tales about her unwanted suitor. She could have complained to her mother, his parents, and others about his leering looks and suggestive comments. Maria prayed for this thorn in her side rather than rail against him. Imitate her reticence. Don't spend time rehashing your child's misdeeds or the nasty remarks she directed at you. Don't harangue your spouse about the character flaws of your stepchild. You, too, can refrain, and forgive. Forgiveness is healing. It washes away the bad feelings, quiets the urge to bad-mouth, and ushers in waves of love.

Transform Expectation into Appreciation

Who is this adolescent, the one with the sarcastic sneer or the snarling mouth? Whatever happened to that sweet child of yours? It's not unusual for you to look at an unpleasant teenager as little more than a composite of repulsive clothes, hairstyles, and tattoos, a fresh mouth, and uncooperative ways. This is not the teenager you imagined you would have, not the person you envisioned when you bounced her on your knee.

When you are so caught up in judging the shortcomings or mistakes of your daughter, you not only lose sight of who that child was, but you also lose sight of who that child is. The good side of her personality, the skills she possesses, the accomplishments she has racked up—when was the last time you tallied these? It is possible that a great deal of a child's rebellion is retaliation. She is lashing out at expectations you have that may not fit her or judgments that she deems unfair. Is it wrong to have expectations? Of course not. We want our children to grow up to be like us, to reflect our values, and to live up to our dreams for them. When they don't go along with our script, it's often trouble.

If you are trying to cope with a rebellious teen, the story of St. Alphonsus Liguori and his father should give you pause and, we hope, a new perspective.

Alphonsus Liguori was born into a noble military family in Naples in 1696. His father was a swashbuckling sea captain, a macho type who prided himself on the assumption that his son would grow up to be just like him. To Papa Liguori's chagrin, young Alphonsus was small and asthmatic, not robust and big boned. He wasn't likely to be the strong, daring military protégé his father so wanted. Luckily, the boy was smart, even brilliant. So Papa adapted his plan for his son's future. He enrolled Alphonsus in the university to study law, and the young man did well.

There was only one problem. Papa saw his son graduating into a prestigious career, and Alphonsus did win a reputation for handling complex cases. Yet the young man's interests remained with the plight of the poor. He dropped out of the legal fast track. Then, while Dad was busy arranging a good marriage, Alphonsus insisted he was too asthmatic for the rigors of spousal love, meaning sex. He wanted to become a priest.

Papa swallowed his disappointment yet again (and probably his doubts about the boy's manhood). But parents are resilient. He considered the advantages of having a bishop vested with religious wealth and power in the family and arranged for his son to study for the priesthood at home. Papa's visions for his son crashed again when Alphonsus insisted that he wanted to be a prelate to the poor and disadvantaged, not the rich.

The young priest lived with the knowledge that he was a failure in his father's eyes. That is a heavy weight for any child to carry through adolescence. He relied on God for guidance. He taught the poor in Naples and reached out to the lowest rung of society. His congregation swelled with converted thieves, murderers, and prostitutes. One stormy night, his father sought refuge in the church and was amazed when he heard his son's wonderful preaching ability. Yet he remained frustrated because this gifted holy man son of his was recognized and appreciated only by the dregs of the community, not by the cream of the crop.

Alphonsus continued his work and gave retreats up in the mountains to the abandoned village people. Eventually, his retreats became so popular that the nobility of the town traveled many miles to attend them. In his community Alphonsus was called a saint for his character and commitment. Finally, his father realized that his son's holiness and dedication, not fame or accomplishment, defined his boy's real success.

St. Alphonsus went on to found the Redemptorist order. He continued to butt heads with his cleric supervisors but never strayed from his desire to be the priest of the poor. His life echoed with a constant theme of rebellion. He and his father were on a collision course for most of their lives. His father fought his life plan and the way he executed it every step of the way. Can you imagine all the conversations his father had over this stubborn, pigheaded son? "My brilliant son threw away a career in law, refused perfectly wonderful women to marry, insisted on a parish in the worst possible part of town. Then, if that wasn't bad enough, he had to head for the hills! What's wrong with that boy? He's determined to be a failure!"

As a parent you can surely see the father's side. Just for a moment, now, take a look through Alphonsus's eyes. He knew his limitations and his own mind. He had a course set for himself.

Ask yourself: *Am I on a collision course with my child?* Is what you want for your child the same as what he wants? If not, could that be at least part of the reason for all the anger and rebellion? If you hate his friends, his look, his music, his preoccupations—are you justified? You may be making it impossible for your child to find any common ground with you. Your expectations may be too narrow—too much yours and not enough his. Such stubbornness on your part could be fueling nasty words and family stalemates. Now ask yourself this: Do I have the son or daughter I wanted? The answer, let's face it, is probably not.

If not, can you accept the son or daughter you have? Her negatives—purple hair, face and body paint—may indeed indicate rebellion, but could they also be expressions of creativity? Try to find what is lovable about your child no matter how truant or defiant she or he is. You wanted him to study art history; to him, art is in the four tattoos on his arm. She appears to you as little more than a shallow party girl, but isn't being social also a talent? Turn around your critique of your child this way and that until you can see the irritating elements in a different light.

Identify what she likes and is good at. How can you help your child realize her dream, not yours? You must discover who your child is, embracing the positives and making peace with negatives. Then tell your child you are committed to helping her realize her dreams, not yours. Tuck her in at night and tell her that you love her no matter what, no matter how bad things have become between you. Tell her that love survives everything, even the teenage years.

This bedtime reassurance is a way to display your love. Our children need to see us demonstrate our love. Haven't they seen enough signs of our disappointment and even disgust?

Transform Heat-of-the-Moment Anger into Love

It is easy to meditate on forgiveness and acceptance in the quiet of a church and to commit to treating your teen differently. Then you come home and find he hasn't taken out the garbage, again—his one and only chore. Or you walk into her room to deliver her laundry, and you can't find one spot that isn't strewn with more dirty clothes, papers, and other debris. Or the telephone breaks your resolves as you hear yet another complaint from a teacher or principal about your child's absence, lateness, or failure.

Each of us has hot buttons. When one is pushed, we explode. For this parent, it was disrespectful talk:

My son is sixteen, and all we seem to do is yell at each other. The other day we were in a department store. He

proceeded to swing back and forth between abusive
anger and desperate apologies because he wanted me to
buy him a shirt. After shelling out for sneakers, I hadn't
the money to indulge him. In front of several horrified
shoppers he cursed at me, saying things like I suck and
he f—— hates me. It wasn't one of my proudest
moments, but he so enraged me that I, too, lost it. I
slapped him in the face. If there is one thing I won't tol-
erate, it's a filthy mouth. For the first time I found myself
despising him.

There are moments like this when your child deserves discipline, yet you must proceed calmly. You want to be a vessel
of love and not a cauldron of frustration. Even the most outra-
geous teen needs our boundaries, but he also needs our love.

One way to master that demonstration of love—especially
in the heat of an argument—is to have an anchor. There is no
better way to anchor yourself than with something concrete.
Resurrect your Catholic jewelry. Did you receive a Miraculous
Medal or a scapular as a gift at your baptism, first communion, or confirmation? Was there a time in your life when you
wore a St. Christopher medal? Is there a golden cross in your
bureau drawer?

Somewhere between our childhood and our children's
childhood, religious jewelry became hollow fashion accessories. Madonna—the rock star, not our Lady—comes to mind.
She co-opted crucifixes and rosaries, raising the chic factor
while tarnishing their sacred essence. Your jewelry and religious accessories probably have been relegated to the recesses
of an old jewelry box. It's time to look for them. If you never
received any of these tokens, it's time to purchase one at a religious articles shop.

If you have one of these medals or cloth adornments pressing against your skin or within reach, you can work God's alchemy instantly with a touch. A medal or cross can be a sensory cue to choose love instead of anger at a moment of frustration. Touching a scapular or a medal can be a gesture toward reaching for forgiveness rather than retaliation and can keep you from lashing out.

THE HISTORY OF RELIGIOUS ORNAMENTATION

You wouldn't be the first to find these anchors helpful to your spiritual well-being. A long history exists behind the use of Catholic jewelry and accessories. Religious medals surfaced in the form of coins. Each was chiseled with a spiritual inscription or image and then fitted to be worn suspended from one's neck. This practice dates back to the early Christian ages. The images of St. Peter and St. Paul decorated early medals, as did those of the martyrs. Christ adorned many coin medals, too, throughout Rome, Constantinople, and even North Africa.

The making and wearing of medals waned during the Middle Ages. Then, around the twelfth century, they reappeared, this time called "pilgrim signs." Certain well-known shrines were celebrated on them, and medals became popular again. In the thirteenth century, medals were renamed "jettons." Jettons bore the initials of the owner and pious mottoes such as "Love God and Praise Him" or "Hail Mary, Mother of God." They were used as tickets, calling cards, and even currency.

The medals familiar to us today can be traced to around the sixteenth century. Metallic images of Jesus and Mary flourished, and the practice of having them blessed is attributed to Pope Pius V. A century later, every city in Europe had its own medal featuring Christ, the Virgin Mary, a favorite saint, or a popular devotion. Let us consider the popular items that Catholics wear.

Hold a Miraculous Medal Close to Your Heart

The Blessed Virgin Mary herself gave us this medal through a French girl named Zoe Labore. Zoe became a member of the Daughters of Charity of St. Vincent de Paul and was known as Sr. Catherine. On July 18, 1830, Sr. Catherine was awakened by a shining child standing in her room. The child led her to the chapel, where Mary waited. They talked for two hours. Four months later, Catherine saw this vision of the Virgin Mary again in the chapel. This time, the Blessed Mother appeared standing on a globe of the world with rays of light streaming from her hands. A slogan encircled her that said, "O Mary, conceived without sin, pray for us who have recourse to you." This vision of Mary revolved so that Catherine could see the back as well. She made out a large letter *M* with a cross and two hearts. One of those hearts bore a crown of thorns. The other was pierced by a sword. Catherine was instructed by Mary to have this image made into a medal. Furthermore, Catherine was told that those who wore the medal would receive many graces and be protected by the Virgin Mother.

Catherine told no one about these clandestine appearances of Mary except her confessor, Fr. M. Aladel. She explained all the details of the medal. In June 1832, with the approval of the archbishop of Paris, the first fifteen hundred medals were created. Soon miraculous events, including healings and changes of heart, happened to many who wore the medal. Wearing the Miraculous Medal, as it came to be called, became a widespread practice among Catholics.

Catherine never told anyone in her convent that it was she who was responsible for the phenomenon. Nor would she appear at any of the hearings examining the apparitions of the Virgin. Not until eight months before her death did Catherine reveal the truth to her superior. In spite of Catherine's privacy and humility, her visions of the Blessed Mother were recognized as official by the church. Catherine was canonized in 1947.

The Miraculous Medal has the power to grant a change of heart. When you feel as if your child is breaking your heart and your spirit, twirl Mary's gift between your fingers. Ask St. Catherine Labore and our Lady to heal your heart with love.

Wear a Scapular, Personal Patchwork of Deliverance

Scapulars have always been vested with messages of deliverance. If you aren't familiar with this religious article, it is a piece of fabric approximately two inches square. The scapular is embroidered or stamped with a picture of our Lady, a particular saint, or the object of a devotion such as the Sacred Heart of Jesus.

The first to wear scapulars were monks, such as the Benedictines and Dominicans. A monk's scapular, long with a hole for the head, was worn over the tunic and across the shoulders, symbolizing the yoke of Christ. That part of the monk's wardrobe served as a constant reminder of his spiritual ideals and tradition. Scapulars had spiritual benefits and were thought to be a protection against hell.

Smaller scapulars were given to laypersons associated with particular orders. Eventually the practice of wearing scapulars reached many Catholics.

One of the most popular is the Green Scapular. Just as the Blessed Mother chose someone to whom to reveal her medal, she selected another Daughter of Charity of St. Vincent de Paul, a woman by the name of Justine Bisqueyburu, to receive her special scapular. Mary visited Justine again and again, until the sister understood what the scapular should look like. This Green Scapular of the Immaculate Heart is inscribed with the words "Immaculate Heart of Mary, pray for us now and at the hour of our death." Mary directed that it can be worn by anyone and should be blessed by a priest. It was approved by Pope Pius IX in 1863. If you wear this scapular, you will receive many graces.

There are some twenty different scapulars. A Brown Scapular (worn in devotion to Our Lady of Mount Carmel) was delivered to St. Simon by the Virgin Mother, according to Carmelite legend. Simon, a religious of the Carmelite order, was on his way home from a pilgrimage in the era of the Crusades when Mary appeared to him and handed him a woolen scapular. During Simon's vision, Mary announced, "This shall be a privilege for you and all Carmelites, that whosoever dies wearing this garment shall not suffer eternal fire; he shall be saved. Wear the scapular devoutly and perseveringly. It is my garment. To be clothed in it means you are continually thinking of me, and I in turn am always thinking of you and helping you to secure eternal life." In time the church extended this scapular privilege to all laypersons who wanted to wear it.

Wearing a scapular was a matter of life and death to Blessed Isidore Bakanja, a twenty-three-year-old Boangi tribesman from the Belgian Congo. A convert to Christianity,

Isidore was ordered to remove his scapular on a February day in 1909. He refused. As a result, he suffered a beating with an elephant hide studded with nails. The infected wounds from this punishing assault festered for six months and killed the young African. Yet as he lay dying, he said, "Certainly I shall pray for him [his abuser]. When I am in heaven, I shall pray for him very much." Like Maria Goretti, Isidore resisted revenge and held on to forgiveness and love. Surely, the scapular played a part in bringing him eternal life as well as death, helping him concentrate on love and not hate.

With many scapulars the theme of deliverance surfaces again and again. Our Lady is an integral part of this religious article. From one mother to another, from one parent to another, her gift helps you become a more loving person and parent. Conversions and cures go hand in hand with the lore of scapulars.

If you feel possessed by ill feelings toward yourself and your child, a scapular can be a tactile reminder that you can be delivered. Just as it did for medieval monks and nuns, it can remind you of your spiritual ideals. When you hold your scapular near your heart, it can inspire you to turn away from evil feelings and toward the love that Mary has for you. Just follow Mary's directions and keep a scapular on your person or among your belongings in your home. Pray to be delivered to love so that you can give it to your child.

In the Cross Fire, Don Your Own Cross

Since Jesus' crucifixion is so central to the Catholic experience, it follows that the cross became a symbol and an object of respect and veneration. Devotion to the cross happened early in the time of St. Paul, one of the original apostles. The cross symbolizes Christ's suffering, but it also came to symbolize the positive message of salvation in God's divine plan. The cross suggests sacrifice but also the source of life—God's love for us. Over the years after Jesus' death, crosses were hung on the walls in homes and places of worship. Stones were engraved with crosses. When the true cross was discovered, devotions increased. Relics were distributed around the world.

The wearing of a cross around your neck can be your personal commitment to celebrating Christ's love and sacrifice for you. Each time you look in the mirror, take a moment to recognize your cross. Get into the habit of really seeing it on your person so you can reflect on it when you and your child are in a cross fire of wills.

By getting into such a routine, a parent like this one can find the answer she's looking for:

> *My thirteen-year-old is so oppositional. I don't want to be around him anymore. I seem to have had it with him and just want him to leave me alone. I try to let go of my resentment, but it's so hard. Now I always assume the worst when he opens his mouth to speak to me. I need to be able to bite my tongue more often so I don't treat him like he treats me. How can I bring out his softer side? And mine?*

Rely on your cross for strength. Give your child a cross to wear as well. Tell him that it is a token of your love and faith in him. This is a loving gesture that your child can understand. When he wears it and sees it, it is the reflection of your reassurance and caring. He will have concrete proof of your love at a time when your relationship doesn't always assure him of that love.

Lighten Your Burden with a
St. Christopher Medal

The legend of St. Christopher will surely resonate with you if your son or daughter has become increasingly harder to handle of late. This third-century martyr originally was known as Offerus. The name suited him; it conjures up his extraordinarily large, burly—dare we say oafish?—size. This girth contributed to his imposing physical strength.

Offerus wanted to align himself with the strongest and bravest leader. Supposedly he first tried a mighty king and even Satan. The king, as it turned out, was afraid of Satan, and the devil became frightened when he saw a cross along the road. A hermit guided Offerus toward Christ.

Offerus took the name Christopher after his baptism. With his wide shoulders and muscled arms and legs, he was given the job of carrying people, and even cattle and horses, across his region's dangerous river. One stormy night, a child appeared at his door and asked to be ferried across the river.

Christopher agreed, surely thinking this was going to be a light and easy task. As soon as his feet touched the water, though, the wind howled, the rain pelted the river, and the water churned fiercely. The child himself seemed to get heavier and heavier. Christopher struggled against the elements and the weight of his charge. He dug deep down into the resources of his strength to get to the other side and place the child safely on the shoreline.

He gasped for breath and felt confused. How could so tiny a child be so incredibly heavy? He asked, "Who are you, child?"

The child told Christopher that he was Christ, the redeemer. He praised the giant for succeeding in a task that was akin to carrying the weight of the world on his back. He told Christopher to put his staff in the ground. Miraculously a palm tree laden with fruit appeared. The miracle converted many, but the notoriety was disastrous for the gentle giant in the long run. He was imprisoned and put to death by pagan leaders.

The symbolism of the giant helping Christ bear the yoke of all worldly trials and tribulations made St. Christopher an extremely popular saint. Throughout Europe his statue became a well-known fixture in many church entrances. A medal bearing his likeness remains popular today.

When your teenager stretches you to your limits, when you feel as if you don't have the strength to go on, press your St. Christopher medal to your chest. Share your burdens with someone who understands. Just as Christopher found the strength, so shall you. Focus on the fact that this saint got to the other side of a choppy river in a howling storm with the child in his care intact. You, too, can do the same. Keep putting one foot in front of the other and aim your eyes on tomorrow. This exercise will fortify you at a moment when you need an extra jolt of strength, patience, and love.

Rely on Love to Get You to the Other Side of Midnight

By making good use of God's inspired medals and crosses and Mary's scapulars, you can transmute negative emotions into love, even if that only means biting your tongue, rewriting a curse into a prayer, or walking away from a confrontation. Rely on any or all of these accessories as your spiritual crutch and conscience. If you have a treasured locket, put a picture of your favorite saint in it. That, too, can be a customized anchor for you.

Anchored in love, you will find ways to handle your child and your negative feelings. Even in a moment of rage, you can postpone a showdown by saying, "Let's cool off and talk about this later, okay?" Even the child who is on a disastrous detour can be approached at a quiet moment and reassured with a reminder like this: "Remember when I was your hero or your whole world? I know things are bad between us now, but someday we'll be all right again."

The alchemy that God is capable of working is boundless. And although it may take longer, you too are capable of alchemy, in your ability to convert your emotions and experiences into love. Rest assured that you have the ability to transmute disappointment, even hate, into love. Your relationship with your child or stepchild may be a miserable one now, but love can work miracles over time.

If you can't find any positives about your teenager, heed this parent's experience:

> I walked down the street, and a young man passed me. I inhaled his cologne. I recognized the fragrance because it's my son's favorite, too. That smell made me sick, because thoughts of my son these days always pain me. My reaction saddened me so. Later that day I was putting up our Christmas tree. I found an ornament my son had made as a child, a Santa colored red and trimmed with cotton balls, affixed with tacks so his arms and legs moved. I remembered the exact moment my son handed that to me. How proud I was of him at that moment. Sitting there, I felt tears roll down my cheeks, tears of love this time.

Rather than allow yourself to wallow in nostalgia and regret, find memories that can transcend time and your current crisis. Go down in your basement, or up to your attic, into your jewelry box, out to your garden, or through your china closet.

There you will find something—an old *Ghostbusters* Halloween mask, a butterfly pin, a rosebush, kindergarten drawings, papier-mâché flowers—a memento from the past that will melt your heart. Tokens such as these can bridge the gap of heartache. Love will nourish you until you reach the other side of this midnight.

LOVE IS A TWO-SIDED COIN

Here is one side of a story and a plea for love sent to us by a teen. She was answered by a story of renewed love. Maybe in these confessions you will see the reflection of your child and, we hope, your future.

The teenage girl wrote to us:

Hi, I'm fifteen. I'm not a mom, but I have one. We do not get along at all. Why? Well, I have messed up in the past year with a lot of drinking. Like the time I got grounded for getting wasted. I got wasted again next time. I know my mom is concerned about my drinking and especially about boys. She's heard rumors (we live in a town that gossips for a hobby) about me and my friends. In fact, those rumors got us into a big fight that even got physical. But I have changed. How do I get my mom to trust me again? She doesn't trust me one bit. What do you do if you are truly sorry for what you did? I have tried in many ways to show my mom that I am more mature now and that I have learned from my mistakes. I'm done with guys for now. I just want to be with my friends. And I just want to make my mom and me get along.

The daughter feels that what's done is done. She wants her mother's love and trust back. How does she get a second chance, a better rapport with a mother who is stuck in distrust and disappointment? This mother needs to look again at her child. Do you need to take another look at your child? Perhaps you need to look ahead to the time when your child will have matured. To help you do that, read the words of this former wild child, sent in response to the young girl above:

> *Only time and proving yourself are key in getting your mom's trust back. Take it from someone who knows firsthand what you are going through. At fifteen, I was you and then some—drinking, drugging, skipping school and failing, sneaking out, and having sex. My mom, a single mother, did all she could to control me. She couldn't. I got pregnant at sixteen. My mom put me in a Christian home for pregnant unwed mothers; I ran away. I went to live with a family I knew from church. To make a long story short, it took time and a lot of proving, but I got my mom's trust back. I'm twenty-five now, and we are best friends. I'm married with a nine-year-old and a new baby. I never knew how much I hurt my mom until I had a child. Your mom is trying to look out for you. She will come around. Don't give up.*

All love stories have two sides. Even the most cantankerous teenager has her side. You, the parent, have yours. All good love stories have ups and downs, comedic moments and tragic times. The one thing that remains constant is that thread of love. When you feel it slipping through your grasp, think back to your child's earlier days. Relive the loving moments. Look forward to that kind of reality again.

In the meantime, keep in mind that all love stories have a hidden theme and an invisible protagonist: God. He is there to refuel your supply of love with his grace. He has provided you with stories of saints, human beings who tapped into his love when they needed it most. Several saints have cooperated with the Virgin Mary to create treasures and tokens to anchor you in the endless bounty of our Savior's love. Wear a token of that love. Ask, and that token will miraculously change your heart.

Nothing is more important than love. Your child can't live without it. You need it. When your child withholds it, go to God for it. In his life and his words, St. Paul (whose story we will read in chapter 2), teaches us how to love and give it priority. In his first letter to the Corinthians, St. Paul said, "Though I command languages both human and angelic—if I speak without love, I am no more than a gong booming or a cymbal clashing. And . . . though I have all the faith necessary to move mountains—if I am without love, I am nothing."

Without love and compassion as coping mechanisms, we parents and our offspring can turn clashing and booming. Love conquers all. Find ways to feel love and to show it to your young adolescent. This can be as simple as preparing your daughter's favorite meal or picking up her room and making her bed so that she comes home to calm, not clutter. Buy her a small token, such as her favorite lip gloss. Say the words "I love you." Touch her even when she rushes by. When you and your child are gripped in big problems, it is in the little things that you can keep the love flowing between you. As you embrace God's love and become filled with it, you will be replenished. Then you can give it to yourself and your child.

Prayer for Charity

Dear Jesus, so often these days I am ready to take your name in vain. At that moment, I promise to whisper your name instead. When I do, I shall look into your sacred heart. I beg you to look into mine. And look into my child's heart, too. Where there is anger and belligerence, change those feelings into love. You are the alchemist who can miraculously make over any hard heart. You can resculpt my emotions. Bless me with the forgiving nature that Maria Goretti and Isidore Bakanja displayed so effortlessly. Flood my angry thoughts with images of your mother, Mary, who will visit me with celestial talismans, just as she visited others like Catherine Labore and Simon. When my heart is cold, warm me with your everlasting love. Replenish my spirit with your charity so that I may pass along your loving legacy to myself and my child. Amen.

Saints Who Can Guide You toward Charity

St. Maria Goretti can help you remember the innocence of forgiveness.

St. Alphonsus Liguori can remind you that all children need to be appreciated for their uniqueness.

St. Catherine Labore and St. Simon can prove to you that the Blessed Mother has special gifts of love for you.

Blessed Isidore Bakanja can urge you to rely on religious tokens to anchor you in love.

St. Christopher can carry you over the abyss of uncharitable thoughts to the safe haven of love.

St. Paul can be counted on as your biblical consultant of love.

Discussion Questions

1. Parenting a teenager who is angry, fresh mouthed, lazy, and sullen can drain you of tender feelings. When faced with acknowledging that you don't like your child, do you feel guilty? Rather than get stuck in a quagmire of guilt, try to understand why your child has become angry, immobilized, or sad. Ask your spouse, and your child, for his or her take.

2. You may feel as if you are on a collision course with your adolescent that is marked by either constant fighting or no communication at all. Can you introduce a truce time? How might you go about doing this? (For example, you could make a rule that the dinner hour is for small talk and catch-up conversations, not for issues or arguments.)

3. Be honest: do all of your child's "sins"—the tattoo, the sleeping till noon, the hanging out with ne'er-do-well compadres—demand repercussions? Are some about taste? Can you see the difference? Can you prioritize your gripes and pick your battles in order to make life better for you and your child?

4. Discipline takes many forms. You can use firm, rational statements and consequences, or you can react emotionally with spur-of-the-moment tirades. Which style do you most often use? If you employ name-calling ("How could you be such an idiot?") or physical means, it's time to rethink your tactics.

5. Do you withhold approval and love, as St. Alphonsus's father did? When was the last time you hugged your teen for no reason,

or kissed him goodnight or good-bye, or commended him for a considerate gesture? What is one seemingly insignificant gesture you could make each week—such as cooking your child's favorite meal, renting a special video, picking up a small gift, or doing a family chore for your child—that would demonstrate your love? Promise yourself that you will try to do this.

6. When you are focused on a child's misbehaviors, you frequently erupt in frustration. What can you do to change your emotional gears so that you resist erupting? One way is to post a holy card of a particular saint, such as Maria Goretti, on your refrigerator. Keep in mind that demonstrating such coping techniques is a way to teach your child how to switch gears as well.

7. If you wear a cross, a scapular, or a Miraculous Medal, look for a window of opportunity to explain its significance to your child. Ask your son or daughter: Would you like me to give you a piece of religious jewelry as a token of my faith in you?

8. Heat-of-the-moment battles trap you in the present. Have you ever stopped to consider that these teenage years are but a few turbulent blips in a relationship that spans a lifetime? Go backward to build a bridge toward better days. How can you relive good memories with your teenager? (For example, peruse photo albums or compile a list of good things your child has done.)

9. Consider the expression "When the going gets tough, the tough get going." How do you respond when your son or daughter acts out? Do you shut down or turn away, or do you recognize that this is when he or she is most in need of your reassurance and care?

10. Does forgiveness come easily to you? Do you hold grudges quietly but relentlessly, or do you let them go? Measuring your capacity for forgiveness is critical while you are parenting a

tempestuous child. Practice forgiving yourself and forgiving your child. Discuss the difference between forgiving an outburst and holding a child accountable for unacceptable or dangerous behavior.

chapter two

Knowledge

*Three things are necessary for the salvation of
man: to know what he ought to believe;
to know what he ought to desire;
and to know what he ought to do.*

—St. Thomas Aquinas

Our quest for wisdom can strengthen our bonds with our children and our belief in God. We cannot make progress on the path to wisdom without acquiring knowledge. Our earthly journey involves learning not only about ourselves, but also about our children. We do this by staying close to them, listening to them, and understanding their needs and issues. Our spiritual journey involves understanding that we are part of the larger kingdom of God. This knowledge will help us confront the challenges we face in every aspect of our life.

Our pursuit of knowledge, both secular and sacred, must continue throughout our lifetime. Yet too many of us live in darkness, failing to learn more about our relationship with God and also neglecting to understand how our relationship with our children should change as they mature.

Parenting education doesn't stop when our children become young adolescents. In fact, gathering knowledge becomes much more critical during these years. Too many of us, however, slow down the learning process as we age. How many times have you resisted learning about new technology— ignoring the Internet, for example, hoping it will go away? How many times have you judged your child by your own experiences as an adolescent, refusing to recognize that our present environment is much more dangerous for young people? Do you try to educate yourself about your child's world, meeting his friends, listening to his music, watching his TV programs, reading about the youth culture? Doing so doesn't mean you must become a present-day Dick Clark, rockin' and rollin' to the beat. But if you never pick up a teen magazine and read what your teen is reading, how will you understand your competition? When your daughter stops eating in a quest to be slim, you might blame your cooking, not the rail-thin stars she has adopted as her role models.

Just as parenting education doesn't stop with our children's adolescence, our religious education doesn't end with confirmation. That might be the last time we are required to study Catholicism and our faith, but it shouldn't be the stopping point for enriching our understanding about our religion.

Why is continuing religious education so important? We relate differently to religion as we age. When we view religion through our own life experiences, we can ferret out deeper meanings that may have eluded us earlier. Consider, for example, the parable of the prodigal son. Jesus told this story as a parable about heaven, his message being that even those sinners who stray far away will be welcomed back into the fold by God. As a child listening to this story, you probably focused on the unconditional love the father had for his son, possibly hoping that your own father would feel the same way if you happened to wander off. Now that you are a parent, no doubt you see this story through the father's eyes, hoping that your child, like the prodigal son, will one day return to you. "Rejoice, because your brother here was dead and has come to life; he was lost and is found." Oh, how you long to utter those words!

We relate differently to our kids as they grow and we get older. Without enough knowledge of them and of ourselves, we fumble around, not knowing where we are or where we are heading. If you are bogged down in the day-to-day trials of dealing with a difficult adolescent, you may feel helpless. You're not. You have two powerful weapons. You have the ability to gather the information you need to assist your child. And you have God. After you have done everything you can, you can leave the rest to him.

When we understand that God lives within each of us, we no longer feel powerless. We know that he is there and that with his guidance, nothing is impossible, even rescuing a troubled child.

HEARING THE GOOD NEWS OF OUR LORD

All knowledge comes from the Lord, and the Bible is the physical presence of that enlightenment. The saints can be our guides in our search for knowledge because they were the first "reporters." In the New Testament, the apostles painstakingly covered the events of their days because they knew the power these words would have on succeeding generations to spread the word of our Lord. Who would believe these miracles if they had not been written down?

The saints make for good guides because they know our struggles. We may be tempted to think of the saints as blind followers, men and women who did what they were told and asked no questions. We forget that the saints were human. Many came to the Lord after suffering desperate times when they questioned their beliefs. St. Thérèse of Lisieux, while on her deathbed, was nearly seduced by atheism. What saved her? She didn't turn away from her doubts but faced them full on. Thus, she found the spiritual strength to survive her crisis of faith, even while she could not muster the physical strength to defeat the tuberculosis that racked her body.

Parents may believe that "ignorance is bliss," that if they do not know what a child is doing and do not intervene, things will work themselves out on their own. This laissez-faire attitude will only lead to more difficult times. It takes strength to confront the truth about a wayward child, just as it took strength for St. Thérèse to face her doubts about her faith. God is well aware of our plight, as he revealed to Joshua: "Have I not told you: Be strong and stand firm? Be fearless and undaunted, for go where you may, Yahweh your God is with you." All we have to do is rely on God to be with us and give us strength.

KNOWLEDGE OF GOD'S PRESENCE

How many times have you felt as if you are struggling alone, as if no one (perhaps not even a parenting partner) understands your agony? If you are a single parent, this suffering may truly be overpowering. When your child was younger, it might have been easier to find others to discuss the trials of parenting. You met these mothers and fathers at the playground, at school, at parent meetings, even on the supermarket checkout line as you bought diapers and formula. Now that you have an adolescent, connecting with these parents is not so easy.

Reach out to others. Reconnect with some of the parents you may have lost touch with. Perhaps one of them is also worrying and would welcome a call. Join a support group. If your child has an alcohol problem, find an Al-Anon/Alateen chapter near you and attend regular meetings. You will find other parents there who share your feelings. Many support groups are also available in cyberspace. America Online and the Web have many message boards where you can share your concerns with others. Along the way, you may find that others can offer sage advice on how to handle your dilemma, perhaps pointing you to resources you didn't know were available. Whatever you do, don't continue to endure alone. You need to fortify yourself so you can find the strength to help your child.

Even if you have trouble finding other parents with whom you can talk, you do not have to go through this alone. God is with you, and knowing this can help fortify your spirit. If you doubt that God is with you, you are in good company. Think of St. Peter, who was put to the test on the Sea of Galilee. After performing the miracle of the loaves and fishes, Jesus went up into the mountains alone to pray. He asked his disciples to get into a boat and go before him across the water to the opposite shore. When Jesus returned, the boat was being tossed about in a stormy sea. Jesus terrified the disciples when he started toward them, walking on water. They thought he was a ghost. Jesus reassured them, but St. Peter called out: "Lord, if it is you, tell me to come to you across the water." The Lord said: "Come." St. Peter got out of the boat and began to walk on the water toward Jesus. But then he faltered and called out, "Lord, save me!" Jesus stretched out his hand and saved him.

"You have so little faith," Jesus exclaimed, "why did you doubt?"

How many of us have doubted, too, believing that God has forsaken us in our misery? "Our lives are full of storms and struggles," says John J. O'Keefe, associate professor of theology at Creighton University. "When we keep our eyes on the Lord, we are fine, but too often we are distracted by the overwhelming size of the storm and the ferocity of the wind and waves. We easily lose heart: God will never deliver us from this."

One mother, who had seen many years of upheaval and unhappiness with her children, said: "I feel like God is up there spitting on me. How else to explain why there is no relief to my problems?" It seemed every day brought to light more distressing facts until despair settled in.

When we feel abandoned, it is important to remember that the rough road to wisdom leads us to God. "We can trust that God will deliver us from every storm because God has a record of fulfilled promises," says O'Keefe. "Jesus, while being the 'exact imprint of God's very being' (Hebrews 1:3), was also fully and completely human. He walked on water not as a god but as a person of faith who trusted absolutely in the power of the Father. Perhaps, by spending time in prayer, we too might learn to trust as Jesus trusted."

It's natural for us to try to control everything in our children's lives, to turn around every failing. But when we cannot accept that some things will work themselves out on their own, we do a disservice to God. We leave nothing to him. God, the all-knowing one, has a plan, and the ultimate wisdom is in knowing this. We can search for knowledge in order to recognize and solve problems. We can struggle to achieve wisdom. Yet we may not be destined to comprehend all the details. Our journey is to try, not give up, as St. Peter did initially, and see that God holds the final logic.

THE POWER OF KNOWLEDGE

Are you the type of person who likes to learn? When introduced to something new, whether it's how to plant a vegetable garden or hit a golf ball, are you willing, even eager, to try it? Or do you react with "Why do I need to learn that? I'm never going to use it"? Has that attitude carried over to your personal relationships? How many opportunities to learn something important about your child have you passed up because you were unwilling to make the effort? At the time it may not have seemed important to spend that extra twenty minutes tucking her in so that she could tell you about her day. You may have given short shrift to family meals because you were worn out from work. What you may have lost was a meaningful conversation with your son.

Now, of course, you wish you had spent more time listening and learning. Perhaps then you wouldn't be so bewildered by your child. It's crucial to gather knowledge about our adolescents, even though we might not have a clue at the time about how we will use the information we gather. We can look to the life of St. Madeleine Sophie Barat for the truth of that statement. This French saint was the quintessential student, spending her entire life learning everything she could. When she began her education, however, she had no idea how useful her knowledge would be later on. Her destiny was to found in France the first Sacred Heart School, which has grown to a worldwide network.

Madeleine Sophie Barat was born in 1779 in Joigny, France, a town in the northwestern corner of Burgundy. Her father, Jacques, a winemaker, was hardworking and reliable, while her mother, Marie-Madeleine, was better educated. Madeleine Sophie combined the best characteristics of both parents. She was intelligent and ambitious, yet had common sense and was well liked by others.

Her parents' influence was great, but the person within her family who had the greatest effect on her was her brother, Louis, eleven years her senior, who was set on a life in the priesthood. When Madeleine Sophie was barely seven, he began to teach her Bible history, the history of France, grammar, arithmetic, physics, and geometry. He required her to learn Spanish, Italian, Latin, and Greek, including memorizing long passages of Homer and Virgil.

Don't get the idea that Madeleine Sophie was an intellectual snob or nerd. When not being educated by her brother, she could be found cavorting with her friends in the vineyards. Still, by the age of ten she had so impressed her pastor that he allowed her to receive Holy Communion—this at a time when children were not allowed to receive this sacrament.

But if all was tranquil inside the Barat household, conditions were tumultuous in France. The antireligious forces in the country had gathered strength and required all members of the clergy to sign a new civil constitution, which would bring the Roman Catholic Church in France under control of the French government. Upon the urging of his family, who feared for his safety, Louis, who was at that time a deacon, signed the paper. Within a few months, however, the pope denounced the paper, Louis recanted his oath, and he was placed in prison.

Louis narrowly escaped death by guillotine and in February 1795 returned to Joigny to be ordained a priest. He found Madeleine Sophie a changed girl. Now fifteen, she had lived through a difficult time. Her family had been forced into hiding several times. During this dark period of her life, she had discovered that only one thing mattered to her: loving and serving God.

Her brother took her to Paris to continue her studies under his direction. With two other young girls, Madeleine Sophie continued her secular studies. Alone, she was put through a much more demanding course in the Scriptures and theology. Mother C. E. Maguire, in her book *Saint Madeleine Sophie Barat,* says, "It was her familiarity with these that gave such solidity and balance to her own spiritual life and to her later teaching, preserving them from every hint of sentimentality and giving an intellectually sound basis for her devotion."

In 1800, Madeleine Sophie discovered a way to use her knowledge. She met Joseph Varin, a priest whose goal was to set up a society of women who would be devoted to the Sacred Heart and teach girls from the higher classes. His motto was "Courage and confidence!" Fr. Varin encouraged Madeleine Sophie to trust herself and what she knew, to have faith in God and follow where he called.

Fr. Varin's influence also touched Madeleine Sophie in another way. When she first devoted herself to the Sacred Heart, she thought about human beings as sinners. Through Fr. Varin, she learned that she could take the information she possessed, interpret it in a different way, and inspire herself and others to view God's message positively. Instead of seeing God's people as sinners, she was able to think about their redemption. In modern parlance, she was able to view the glass as half full rather than half empty. Madeleine Sophie's upbeat attitude would prove integral to her success as an educator and leader. She encouraged others to view the Sacred Heart as a symbol of Christ's love and compassion. With her guidance, the girls and young women who studied at her school focused not on the fires of hell, but on the fire coming from the Sacred Heart.

Take a page from Madeleine Sophie's textbook when dealing with your child. If your young adolescent has hit a rough patch, she may have destroyed the trust you once had in her. Your tendency may be to always regard events negatively, never finding any positive developments that could signify that things are turning around. Ask for Madeleine Sophie's help that you may try not to judge each situation based on past information. Gather new knowledge and look at the situation with a fresh eye.

Sharing Knowledge with Others

Saints like Madeleine Sophie Barat knew it was not enough to possess knowledge—they had to articulate their beliefs to others in order to convert them to their way of thinking. Parents quickly learn that this is a hard task to perform with adolescents because they can be great debaters. Before you confront your young adolescent about any matter, be ready to outline and defend your point of view.

Learn from the experiences of St. Catherine of Alexandria, a fourth-century pagan princess from Egypt. Because Catherine belonged to a wealthy family, she had the opportunity to study. She learned about Christianity and became intrigued. One night while sleeping, she had a vision of the Virgin and Child. The next day, she became a Christian.

Only eighteen and very beautiful, Catherine was courted by many suitors. The most powerful was the Roman emperor Maxentius, who had begun persecuting Christians. As the legend goes, she went to him to ask him to stop his tortures. Her arguments for Christianity were so well thought out and powerful that Maxentius found himself ill equipped to defend his own gods. He called his best philosophers to oppose her. Catherine ended up converting them. Angered, Maxentius had all the philosophers put to death.

He tried to tempt Catherine with the offer of a consort's crown (he was already married). She refused, and he had her imprisoned. While she was confined, Maxentius sent others to break her down. Instead, her reasoning continued to win over new Christians, including Maxentius's own wife.

Now furious beyond belief, Maxentius had Catherine tied to a wheel that was outfitted with sharp spikes. That is why we often see this saint pictured with a wheel. Maxentius intended to use it to torture Catherine to death, but a miraculous thing happened. The wheel broke apart, its spikes shooting out and injuring some of the bystanders. Not to be stopped, Maxentius had her beheaded. Milk, not blood, flowed from her wounds after her death.

St. Catherine discovered that her words, no matter how enlightened, sometimes fell on hostile ears. What parent has not had that experience! Who knows whether the presence of God himself would have been enough to sway Maxentius from his pagan beliefs? The resistance Catherine encountered, however, did not deter her from her path. She remained resolute and faithful to God, knowing that his was the true word. Today we would say that she had the courage of her convictions, and she certainly was not the only saint to display such bravery in the face of deadly threats.

We can pray to St. Catherine to give us strength to withstand the criticism of our children or others as we work our way through our problems. One parent who wrote to us may have found some small encouragement in the story of St. Catherine. She wrote:

We sent our daughter to a wilderness program because she was using drugs and had become very rebellious. We educated ourselves beforehand and felt this therapeutic environment was exactly what she needed to get back on track. Imagine our surprise when the father of one of her friends began to openly criticize us for our action. He told my daughter's friends that we should be arrested for child abuse! We were in such pain having our daughter away. It was the hardest thing we've ever had to do. But to have this father condemn us without knowing the facts—we were wounded beyond belief.

St. John the Baptist could empathize with this parent's plight. Here was a saint who suffered endless ridicule during his lifetime. He often exiled himself to the desert to think and pray and live on grasshoppers. This fate seems an odd one for a man with all the right family connections. His mother was Elizabeth, Mary's cousin, who said to Mary, "Blessed is the fruit of your womb," as recorded in the Scriptures by Luke.

Yet John set himself on a tough path that flouted contemporary beliefs and made him a target for hatred. John's mission was to pave the way for Christ. And in that, he did a marvelous job. Remember, he lived in pagan times, when the idea of one true God was anathema to religious beliefs. He preached the coming of Christ while telling men and women to wash away their sins with the tears of penitence. When people came to him, ready to repent, he baptized them in the river. Soon some of the Jews began to look upon him as the Messiah, a claim he hastened to deny, saying that while he baptized with water, the true Messiah would baptize with the Holy Spirit.

John was not afraid to speak out against wrongdoing. He criticized Herod, who had put away his wife and was living with Herodias, who was both his niece and the wife of his half brother. Herodias, stung by John's criticism, vowed her revenge. She convinced Herod to imprison the saint.

On the occasion of a great feast, Salome, Herodias's daughter by her lawful husband, danced for Herod and so pleased him that he offered to grant her any favor. Urged on by her mother, Salome asked for the head of John the Baptist on a platter. While startled by the request, Herod felt he could not refuse and sent his guards to John's cell to cut off his head. When the soldiers returned with John's head on a dish, Salome grandly presented it to her mother. Jesus, upon being told of John's death, retreated to the desert to pray.

John the Baptist paid the ultimate price for his beliefs. His lifestyle made him an outcast, and his contemporaries questioned his judgment. Yet he remained steadfast on the course he chose. Similarly, parents pushed to rescue an out-of-control adolescent may be ostracized by others. They should ask John the Baptist to strengthen their resolve, knowing that they are acting out of love.

Guiding with a Gentle Hand

Do you sometimes feel overwhelmed with too much information? Then pray to St. Bonaventure to keep you focused on what is truly important. St. Bonaventure was able to sift through information, separating the relevant facts from the superfluous in order to arrive at sensible conclusions. As a result, when he made a decision, it was based on solid judgment, not guesswork. If you are trying to make decisions about how you should handle your troubled adolescent, ask St. Bonaventure for guidance.

It's important to find a balance with knowledge—you can't become paralyzed when you feel overwhelmed with information, and you can't be heavy-handed in using your knowledge, either. This trap is an easy one for parents to fall into, filling lectures to our children with angry, condescending, and vitriolic words. Rather than empathizing with our children's situation as they navigate a difficult adolescence, we levy harsh judgments that demean their character and damage their self-esteem. We can and should do better.

Learn from St. Bernard. Of noble birth, Bernard was drawn to learning, first because of his shyness, then because of his love of knowledge. One Christmas Eve, he had a vision of Jesus as a newborn infant in the manger. Bernard decided to dedicate himself to the religious life.

Bernard was an appealing preacher. He was young, attractive, wealthy, friendly, witty, and easygoing. He had what we today would term "charisma," that unique blend of talent and charm that makes a person irresistible to others. Despite the fact that he knew he wanted to preach about Jesus, he didn't know how to accomplish that goal. He heard about a Benedictine monastery at Cîteaux, a strict society of monks. He asked God for guidance and decided to opt for the severe life of a Cistercian monk.

After three years at Cîteaux, Bernard was sent to another area of France, Langres in Champagne, along with twelve other monks, to found another house. Here, Bernard and his fellow monks lived through a period of great austerity, with little to eat. Rather than let up on the other monks, however, Bernard came down on them even harder. He reprimanded them for the slightest infraction, whether these missteps came to his attention during the day-to-day running of the monastery or during confession. The effect was not what he had hoped for. Rather than inspire them, he discouraged them. Some young men left, and their numbers dwindled.

Bernard soon realized the error of his ways. He was willing to admit that despite his great knowledge and position of authority, he was wrong. He began to lead with a gentler hand, and his followers responded and grew in number.

Bernard performed many miracles during his lifetime. He restored a lord's speech so that he could confess his sins before he died. The miracle most often associated with him involves flies that infested the church of Foigny. Bernard decreed that the bugs were excommunicated, and they all died. This became a famous tale told in France. Bernard also resolved a number of conflicts in the church. Known as the "oracle of Christendom" for his knowledge and wisdom, Bernard was often called upon by royalty and church leaders for his insight. Perhaps his most famous deed was resolving the papal schism that followed the papal election of 1130.

Bernard learned through his experience with the monks that leading with a gentle hand and a ready ear is the way to go. As parents, we may discover that a similar approach works wonders, even miracles, with our children.

Overcoming Our Fear of Knowledge

Any parent who has ever discovered that a child is using drugs, stealing, or vandalizing neighbors' properties has suffered pain. We have heard many cries of anguish from parents who have stumbled on the truth about a son or daughter and wished they hadn't.

One such incident involved fifteen-year-old Veronica, who was dating Keith, a seventeen-year-old who had been in trouble with the law and was under house arrest. Her parents suspected they were having sex, although Veronica wouldn't talk about it. Her parents were afraid to confront her, afraid their fears would be confirmed. At the same time, Veronica was afraid to tell her parents what was happening, afraid they would condemn her.

Her parents took the lead and began the discussion in a nonconfrontational way, talking about protection and why it was best to wait for someone special. "We kept our cool," her mother said.

At first she denied everything. But then the tears started to roll down her face, and she confessed everything. We had the best talk we had ever had in our lives. She really listened to us. We discussed how her life would change if she had a baby. How Keith would be in her life forever, even if she did not want him there, because this baby would always be there. We talked about STDs and the dangers. We remained calm but let her know that she was loved and we only wanted her to be happy and healthy.

"I have my daughter back, and it is a wonderful feeling," the mother wrote in a later e-mail. "She made me a birthday card and wrote, 'I put you through a lot, and I'm sorry. I love you so much. Thanks for staying on my side.'"

This mother found the courage to face her child's situation. If you are afraid to confront your child, pray to St. Joan of Arc that you may find the strength to do so. This saint had to muster the courage to face God's plan for her life.

Joan was just a young child when disaster struck her homeland. The French king, Charles VI, was insane. The country was embroiled in a civil war that left it unable to counter a real threat from abroad. England's King Henry V took advantage of this unrest to conquer France.

Joan was only fourteen when she began to hear voices that would foretell her destiny. At first, she denied them.

(How many times have we been in this position, seeing the signs but failing to acknowledge them?) But the voices and the visions became so overwhelming that she had no choice but to recognize them for what they were: a call to arms for her to defend her country.

Where were these voices coming from? Joan eventually identified them as St. Michael the archangel, St. Catherine of Alexandria, and St. Margaret of Antioch. They were specific in their instructions. She was to travel to the beleaguered city of Orléans and recapture it from the English—a tall order for a peasant girl who could neither ride nor shoot and had never been in the army, let alone led one. But the voices grew more insistent, and she realized she had no choice but to do what they said.

Along the way, she faced many people who believed her to be an opportunist, a traitor, or a lunatic. Many theologians questioned her. She was able to stand her ground, answering their questions and even, in one case, predicting the outcome of a battle. Finally, Charles VII, heir to the French throne, allowed her to lead his armies. On July 17, 1429, four months after she had presented herself to Charles, she stood by as he was crowned.

She continued to battle for France, but on May 23, 1430, she was captured by the English. The French did nothing to save her. She was left to defend herself on her own.

The English sentenced her as a heretic and a sorceress. A year later, when she was only nineteen, she was burned at the stake.

Joan followed her own voices, her own path, and was certainly viewed during her times as a rebel. Imagine the pain and fear she was compelled to overcome as she lived out her destiny.

Just as Joan first denied the voices she heard, you may be ignoring an instinct that something is seriously wrong with your child. That's understandable. But once Joan acknowledged the voices, she knew she must act. If you can admit that there is a problem with your child, the next step is to do something about it. During such times, ask Joan for guidance. If necessary, she will prod you to move forward.

Nothing Is Impossible with God

When we possess the true knowledge of God and trust in his power, we can muster the courage to face even the most heartbreaking situation. We can understand that anything is possible, even rescuing an adolescent set on a course of self-destruction. The Lord has faced tougher cases, namely, St. Paul.

Early on, Paul, who as a Jew was known as Saul, was a passionate enemy of Christ. He had taken part in the murder of St. Stephen. While St. Stephen has been recognized as the first martyr, his lasting legacy may be that he set in motion the chain of events that would lead St. Paul to Christ. St. Augustine commented, "If Stephen had not prayed, the Church would never have had Paul."

St. Stephen was stoned to death, and Saul was the one who held Stephen's garments. He asked the high priest for a commission to arrest all the Jews at Damascus who were bold enough to profess their belief in Jesus. His request was granted, and he set out on his mission with the intention of bringing the Jews he arrested back to Jerusalem.

When Saul neared his destination, he was surrounded by a bright light. He heard Jesus' voice asking him why he was set against him. Overcome, Saul found that he could not see and had to be guided by others to Damascus. There he stayed in darkness and neither ate nor drank anything for three days. Jesus sent a man named Ananias to restore Saul's sight, and he was baptized.

Saul stayed in Damascus to preach that Jesus was the Son of God. Imagine the astonishment of those who had known Saul as the persecutor, not the defender. Needless to say, the other disciples were wary of Saul, and he had to earn their trust. He made many journeys to preach the gospel, and, of course, his writings form an integral part of the New Testament. Paul, as he was renamed, continued to preach the gospel for many years, until he was arrested in Jerusalem and taken back to Rome, where he was beheaded.

In the Bible, in his letter to the Ephesians, Paul reflects on the amazing nature of his conversion: "I, who am less than the least of all God's holy people, have been entrusted with this special grace, of proclaiming to the gentiles the unfathomable treasure of Christ and of throwing light on the inner workings of the mystery kept hidden through all the ages in God, the Creator of everything." Later, when he recognized his impending death, he wrote in his second letter to Timothy: "My life is already being poured away as a libation, and the time has come for me to depart. I have fought the good fight to the end; I have run the race to the finish; I have kept the faith." His journey was truly remarkable, a story that reminds us that all is possible with God—even those things that seem most impossible.

RECORDING THE KNOWLEDGE OF YOUR JOURNEY

Besides the apostles, many saints spent their lifetime writing down their thoughts about Christ and reflecting on the spiritual trials they suffered. These exposés have proved invaluable to scholars and are precious to us because they provide a road map of the spiritual journeys taken by others. We can be inspired and receive strength from reading their words.

At the same time, your own religious travels are unique. No one else, whether saint or sinner, has been where you have been or will go where you will go. That should be a powerful enough reason to put pen to paper and write about what you are enduring.

You may be thinking your tale is too unimportant to document. St. Thérèse of Lisieux felt the same way about her life. Others did, too: when she lay dying, the nuns in her convent discussed what they could possibly say in her obituary. There was nothing remarkable about her life.

She was one of five surviving children of a watchmaker and his wife. Except for one trip to Rome, she never ventured more than twenty miles from her home. She entered the Carmelite convent when she was only fifteen, and she died when she was twenty-four. She never realized her dream to be a missionary nun to Vietnam. So how did she become so well-known? Thérèse's mother superior had ordered her to write down her life story, probably because she had a vision that this quiet nun was on the road to sainthood. In 1898, a year after Thérèse's death, her autobiography, *The Story of a Soul,* was published with an initial printing of two thousand copies. Most of these were passed out to Carmelite nuns in other convents, but word of mouth took over, and soon people everywhere were clamoring to read about Thérèse. *The Story of a Soul* remains a best seller and has spawned many books written by religious who continue to read and interpret Thérèse's writings. (Go into the bookshop across from St. Patrick's Cathedral in New York, and you will find a whole bookcase devoted to books about Thérèse, with *The Story of a Soul* given the most prominent spot.)

Why is *The Story of a Soul* such a hit? Thérèse comes across very much as the young woman she was, with anxieties, moods, and a sense of humor about herself and God. "We are living now in an age of inventions, and we no longer have to take the trouble of climbing stairs, for, in the homes of the rich, an elevator has replaced these very successfully," she wrote. "I wanted to find an elevator which would raise me to Jesus, for I am too small to climb the rough stairway of perfection." Those of us reading about Thérèse today can see that she is a present-day saint, accessible to us in our modern world.

Perhaps Thérèse's most appealing trait was her humanity, which came across when she admitted her self-doubt and, most of all, her faltering faith. The most ominous period of her life came when she was terribly ill with tuberculosis. She was put through a trial of faith that plunged her into a dark hole of despair, had her contemplating suicide, and found her questioning her belief in God. She flirted with atheism. It seemed the more knowledge she gathered about God and her religion, the more difficult it became for her to believe. She talked about a fog surrounding her: "It penetrates my soul and envelops it in such a way that it is impossible to discover within it the sweet image of my Fatherland; everything has disappeared!"

Ironically, Thérèse's struggle occurred during the Easter season, when she was normally filled with great joy. "During those joyful days of the Easter Season, Jesus made me feel that there were really souls who have no faith, and who, through the abuse of grace, lost this precious treasure, the source of the only real and pure joys," she wrote. "He permitted my soul to be invaded by the thickest darkness, and that the thought of heaven, up until then so sweet to me, be no longer anything but the cause of struggle and torment." Thérèse's trial lasted, in her words, "until the hour set by God Himself and this hour has not yet come."

Reading this passage, we can feel Thérèse's sorrow. But her courage was immense. She didn't run away from the knowledge that she was losing her faith. She embraced it and even prayed for other atheists, knowing how empty their lives were without belief in God.

We have no idea how many people have been consoled during desperate times by reading Thérèse's words. Perhaps you, too, may be helped by knowing that you are not the only Catholic who has doubted the very existence of God in the midst of your sufferings. Take the example of St. Thérèse as inspiration to write down your own thoughts in the hope that they may help others.

Rediscovering the Bible

There was a time when a family Bible could be found in every Catholic's home. It was where you stored the family's birth, marriage, and baptism certificates. Usually it was displayed in a prominent area and was often taken out and read on special holy occasions. Many a child was told in catechism class that dying without reading the Bible meant certain descent into hell.

These days your family Bible (if indeed you have one) may have been relegated to a top shelf. It's time to retrieve it. Now, more than ever, these stories have relevance for your life and can help you understand that your problems, while overwhelming to you right now, have been experienced by others as far back as biblical times.

The stories in the Bible are spellbinding, filled with action, adventure, intrigue, treachery, and humor. Perhaps you have never thought about the Bible as a page-turner, but it can be. Even though we have heard some of these stories before, their majestic language, insight into the human spirit, eloquent descriptions, and overview of history inevitably prove compelling. Many of the phrases that we find sprinkled throughout its pages are familiar. Who hasn't used the expression "salt of the earth" to describe someone who is unpretentious and dependable? Did you know that that saying is from the Sermon on the Mount? The passage reads: "You are salt for the earth. But if salt loses its taste, what can make it salty again? It is good for nothing, and can only be thrown out to be trampled under people's feet" (Matthew 5:13).

Have you ever heard someone tell another person not to "hide their light under a bushel basket," meaning not to cover up their talents? That saying also is from the Sermon on the Mount. This is the passage: "You are light for the world. A city built on a hill-top cannot be hidden. No one lights a lamp to put it under a tub; they put it on the lamp-stand where it shines for everyone in the house. In the same way your light must shine in people's sight, so that, seeing your good works, they may give praise to your Father in heaven" (Matthew 5:14–16).

In fact, the Sermon on the Mount may be the best speech ever written. And Christ's words may have particular relevance to you now. Reflect on the following passages:

"Can any of you, however much you worry, add one single cubit to your span of life?" (Matthew 6:27). The answer, of course, is no. How many times do we need to remind ourselves of this fact when waiting for a child who has missed a curfew?

"Do not judge, and you will not be judged; because the judgments you give are the judgments you will get, and the standard you use will be the standard used for you" (Matthew

7:1–2). Do we find ourselves critical of our children, our parenting partner, other parents?

"Ask, and it will be given to you; search, and you will find; knock, and the door will be opened to you" (Matthew 7:7). We need to include our petitions in our prayers to our Lord.

"So you always treat others as you would like them to treat you; that is the Law and the Prophets" (Matthew 7:12). Those should be the words we live by every day, particularly with regard to our children.

"Enter by the narrow gate, since the road that leads to destruction is wide and spacious, and many take it; but it is a narrow gate and a hard road that leads to life, and only a few find it" (Matthew 7:13–14). We can draw comfort from this that the road we are attempting to follow is the right one. Hopefully, our children will follow.

"Beware of false prophets who come to you disguised as sheep but underneath are ravenous wolves" (Matthew 7:15). We need to pass these words on to our children, who may be led astray by friends.

If you have neglected the Bible recently, now is the time to rediscover the Good News between its covers. First, of course, you need to locate your copy or, if you don't have one, buy one. You may be overwhelmed by the choices in a bookstore or online—type in "Bible" on Amazon.com, and you will be presented with thirty-two thousand choices. Many of these, however, are not the full version of the Bible but versions that focus on particular sections or writers. In the day and age when catchy titles sell books, you will find *10 Ways to Get into the New Testament: A Teenager's Guide; 101 Fun Bible Crosswords; 1,001 Things You Always Wanted to Know about the Bible (but Never Thought to Ask);* and many others.

Start with the original best seller, the Bible. You will discover that there are many versions of this, too. The most
popular for Catholics are the New Jerusalem Bible and the
New American Bible. If you are confused when confronted
with all the choices, ask your parish priest for guidance.
To many of us, picking up a huge Bible and just plunging
in seems like a daunting task. That may even be one reason
you no longer are drawn to its pages. You find its size intimidating and wonder how you will ever find anything meaningful for yourself in a tome of more than one thousand
pages. Our advice is to start small, with a specific story or
passage that is familiar to you. Listen to the readings the next
time you attend Mass, and make note of where they came
from in the Bible. You can later follow up by reading the
fuller account.

You may find some passages that directly relate to your
parenting struggles, such as this one from the second letter of
Paul to the Corinthians: "That is why we do not waver;
indeed, though this outer human nature of ours may be
falling into decay, at the same time our inner human nature is
renewed day by day. The temporary, light burden of our hardships is earning us for ever an utterly incomparable, eternal
weight of glory, since what we aim for is not visible but invisible. Visible things are transitory, but invisible things eternal"
(2 Corinthians 4:16–18).

What we see each day may be a child who is out of control. What we don't see are God's love and the plan he has for
us and our loved ones. We need to refresh our spiritual
knowledge every day to remind ourselves of his love.
Through studying the lives of the saints, their trials and tribulations, we can acquire the strength to confront the painful
circumstances we tend to avoid. The lives of the saints can

lead us across a spiritual bridge from painful knowledge to wisdom by helping us put this knowledge into perspective.

Prayer for Knowledge

Dear Lord, you are the fountain of all knowledge. Everything I know begins and ends with you. I can never hope to absorb all you have to teach me. Like St. Joan of Arc, I feel ill equipped to take on the huge task laid out before me. Like St. Thérèse, I feel like a small child whose faith, at this important juncture, is failing her. Help me learn all I can about you so that I can become like St. Catherine of Alexandria, one of your strong supporters and followers. I pray that others will want to follow my lead, rejecting the road to damnation to choose the gateway to life with you in heaven. Amen.

Saints Who Can Help You Seek Knowledge

St. Madeleine Sophie Barat can help you learn for learning's sake.

St. Catherine of Alexandria can encourage you to express your beliefs persuasively.

St. Joan of Arc can empower you to go where God leads.

St. John the Baptist can console you when others are critical of you.

St. Peter can help you renew your faith in God.

St. Paul can reassure you that even the wicked can be saved.

St. Bonaventure can teach you to filter out what is unimportant.

St. Bernard's example can show you ways to be more empathetic.

St. Thérèse of Lisieux can inspire you to record your own spiritual journeys.

Discussion Questions

1. Learning about our religion shouldn't stop with confirmation. What was the last book or article you read that increased your understanding of Catholicism? How has this knowledge affected the way you practice your faith? The way you parent your child?

2. When Jesus asked St. Peter to walk across the water to him, St. Peter's earthly knowledge—that water is not solid, and therefore he would sink—prevented him from trusting Jesus. Can you think of an occasion when you were unable to trust your child because of past infractions and were proven wrong? What did you learn from that incident?

3. To increase our parenting knowledge, we need to reach out to others. What prevents you from doing so: lack of time, fear of being rejected, difficulty finding new resources? What strategies can you develop to help you find supporters?

4. How do you keep up with the youth culture? Discuss what you have found and how it has helped you understand your child's world.

5. Madeleine Sophie Barat did not know how the knowledge she acquired through her studies would help her in the future, yet she dedicated her life to learning more. How do you react when you encounter information that seems totally irrelevant

to your life? How can you become more like Madeleine Sophie, taking in knowledge regardless of how unimportant it seems at the time?

6. St. Catherine of Alexandria discovered that the Roman emperor Maxentius could not be converted to her way of thinking. If your verbal powers fail with your child, what other methods can you use to get your message heard?

7. St. John the Baptist came from a wealthy family, yet he rejected his family's riches to travel the countryside dressed as a beggar. If you are parenting a modern-day John the Baptist, a child whose dress and unconventional beliefs upset you, what steps can you take to overlook the superficial appearances and uncover your child's deeper feelings?

8. St. Bernard's harsh methods for dealing with subordinates threatened to drive well-meaning people away. Can you remember a time when your harsh manner or words drove your child away? How can you change your behavior so your child will be more cooperative?

9. Sometimes too much knowledge is a dangerous thing. Have you ever spied on your child—searched a backpack, read a diary, checked e-mails, listened to phone conversations—and then felt sorry you did? How could you go about obtaining information in the future without snooping?

10. St. Thérèse of Lisieux thought the story of her religious life was mundane, but it became an international best seller. No life is unimportant. If you wrote the story of your religious life, what would you call it? What would be the lesson others would learn from it?

chapter three

Faith

We are never truly blind, if we see God!

—St. Clare of Assisi

Parenting is inextricably linked with faith. We need to have faith in our abilities to parent. We need to have faith that our children will ultimately learn the lessons we have been teaching them. Above all, we need to have faith in God, that he will watch over us all and guide us.

Somehow, during difficult times in parenting, faith eludes us. We doubt ourselves. We doubt our children. We doubt that God is there for us. Without faith, we become suspicious and anxious. When we can no longer trust our abilities, we second-guess every decision we make, sending mixed signals to our children. When we don't trust our children, we undermine their confidence and give them reasons to rebel. And when we don't trust God, we close ourselves off from his love.

Faith is a gift from God. Each of us, born in his image, is given that faith at birth. But many of us, buffeted by life's misfortunes, have lost our faith along the way. In this chapter, we will offer ways to rediscover faith. We will focus on saints, like St. Lucy and St. Catherine of Siena, who can teach us about faith. We will offer simple suggestions for how you can strengthen your faith day by day. Placing a statue or picture of a favorite saint in your home can help you reflect on your faith during the day. Recovering the sights, sounds, and smells of your childhood faith can be a powerful way of reminding yourself of the beliefs you have forgotten. Music from a time in your past, and even the smell of a burning candle, can bring back memories of praying with childlike innocence in a quiet church. Throughout these exercises, the saints once again will be our constant companions.

Most of us think that faith and sainthood go hand in hand. But many of the saints suffered a crisis of faith at some time during their lives. Perhaps the best example of this is St. Thomas. Absent on the night our Lord appeared to the apostles, Thomas refused to believe that Jesus had risen from the dead. Eight days later, when the apostles were once again together in a locked room, Christ reappeared. After greeting them, he turned to Thomas and said, "Put your finger here; look, here are my hands. Give me your hand; put it into my side. Do not be unbelieving anymore but believe." Thomas fell at his feet exclaiming, "My Lord and my God!" Jesus answered him, "You believe because you can see me. Blessed are those who have not seen and yet believe" (John 20:27–29).

Most of us, like Thomas, have trouble accepting what we cannot see. Unlike Thomas, most of us will not see Jesus, Mary, or one of the saints while we are here on earth. We have to trust our faith that God is watching over us, that he has a plan for our lives, as well as the lives of our children, and that, ultimately, we will all find peace in his presence.

Taking a Leap of Faith

What is faith? The dictionary defines it as "unquestioning belief that does not require proof or evidence." Whether we are aware of it or not, we demonstrate faith many times during our normal day. Some things we believe unquestioningly because they always occur on schedule. We believe that the sun will rise in the morning and set at night. We believe that our car will start when we turn the key in the ignition, that the postal employee will deliver our mail, and that our favorite TV program will be shown at nine o'clock on Monday night. What happens when something goes off kilter? If our engine won't turn over, we may lose faith in the car manufacturer or our mechanic. When our must-see television show is canceled, we may no longer believe the network has our best interests in mind.

We have faith as well in things that aren't as inconsequential as the mail being delivered or a TV program being shown. When we ride a roller coaster, we have faith that the cars will stay on the tracks. We trust that if a fire erupts in our home, the fire department will show up on time. And when someone in our family is sick, we place our fate in the hands of doctors and nurses, having faith that their education, skill, and training will allow them to handle whatever medical crisis they encounter.

In most of these situations, our faith is rewarded with physical results. We can see, hear, or feel the outcome. The sun rises or sets. The mail is delivered, the car starts, the roller coaster doesn't crash. It is more difficult to have faith, to truly believe, in something when it is beyond our grasp. This is what some call "blind faith." In some ways we are blind when it comes to our religious faith. We must believe without seeing.

Some people, even a saint like Thomas, can never master that feat. Others, however, seem to have bottomless reserves of faith that they can draw on no matter what crisis befalls them. Rose Kennedy, the matriarch of the Kennedy clan, was well-known for her resolute faith in God despite having lost so many children and grandchildren to early and violent deaths. Coretta Scott King, widow of Martin Luther King Jr., is another example of someone with steadfast faith.

If we look, we can witness acts of faith happening around us each day. A priest in a New York City parish received a visit from a wealthy man whose wife had died. Although the man wasn't Catholic, his wife was devout. Before she died, she asked him to make a contribution to a Catholic charity. Could the priest suggest a worthwhile cause? The priest recommended a hospice for cancer victims that took no money from the patients, their families, or even government sources. Somehow, God always provided the hospice with the resources it needed.

On taking a tour of the facility, the man was impressed and told the nun who had been showing him around, "This is where I want my money to go." He was touched by the gentle nature of the nuns, who gave so much of themselves to these sick people. He asked the nun what kind of retirement program would provide for them when they needed care. The nun laughed, pointed skyward, and said, "The one upstairs."

That is ultimate faith: the belief that somehow God will prove to be more valuable than a 401(k). These religious women chose to build up their heavenly bank account, having faith that when the time came God would pay them back with interest.

Sometimes the demonstrations of faith we see or read about involve visions. In September 2000, a small apartment in Perth Amboy, New Jersey, was transformed into a shrine when people began to see an apparition of the Virgin of Guadalupe on the glass of one of the windows. Soon a trickle of people became a torrent. People came from miles away, waited in line, and trudged up the steps to leave candles, kneel, say the rosary, ask for a miracle. One teacher who visited summed up the ardor of the pilgrims: "Anything is possible if you have faith. If it is true and you've touched it, you've touched something holy, like a relic."

What separates the faithful from the faithless? Having faith involves the willingness to surrender control to God.

Small children have no control over their lives and must depend upon the adults around them for their care. Perhaps that is why small children have no difficulty believing in Santa Claus, the Easter bunny, or angels. In their innocence, anything seems possible.

Many adults, however, have lost that purity of heart. They do not trust others but strive to control everything in their lives, including their children. They will never truly have certain faith in God. We must trust him to have the answers, even if we don't understand the outcome while we are here on earth. Sometimes people lose faith when they feel they are being punished. But God doesn't hand out punishments here on earth. We can't blame him if we lose a job, suffer a beating in the stock market, or fail to win the lottery. And we shouldn't blame him because we are parenting a difficult child. We behave arrogantly when we ask God for a favor and then turn angry and petulant when our needs are not met. God answers our prayers in his own time, in his own way. Our faith should extend to leaving the results in his hands.

We realize the enormity of the task before us, particularly at this juncture. Perhaps you feel that it has never been more difficult for you to summon the courage to have faith in God. How many times have you asked yourself, *Why me?* Why have you been handed this burden at this time in your life?

We can't give you those answers. What we can do is introduce you to several saints whose faith was sorely tested. They were human, and many of them had doubts. In the end, they relinquished control and trusted in God. We have mapped out five steps that can help you walk in the footsteps of the saints. They can help you regain the faith you may have lost during these trying times.

STEP ONE: KEEP YOUR FOCUS
ON THE FINAL OUTCOME,
SALVATION WITH GOD

Our first step is to remove ourselves from the seeming quagmire of the present and look forward to what awaits us in the future. For inspiration we can pray to St. Lucy, who was born in Sicily during the third century. No matter what obstacles were placed in her path, she regarded them as opportunities for further growth and demonstration of her faith. Throughout her life, she kept her eyes focused on her final reward: rejoicing in the hereafter with our Lord.

Lucy's parents were wealthy, and her father died when she was quite young. Lucy had been raised a Christian, but her mother, Eutychia, encouraged her to marry a rich suitor who was a pagan. Lucy did not tell her mother that she was resolved to remain a virgin. She knew how this news would distress her mother. However, her mother would be won over in a most unexpected way.

Eutychia suffered from a hemorrhage. Lucy suggested that they travel to Catania in Sicily, where St. Agatha had been martyred, and pray to her for a cure. Their prayers were answered, and Eutychia, viewing Lucy's faith with gratitude, encouraged her daughter to pursue her destiny. Lucy's suitor, however, was not so magnanimous. Furious, he accused her of being a Christian and left her to the mercy of a cruel pagan judge. The judge sentenced her to life as a prostitute in a brothel, a punishment she would find repugnant because of her vow of chastity. Yet when the guards attempted to take her away, they found her rooted to the spot. A subsequent move to burn her failed also. She was finally killed when one of the soldiers thrust a sword into her throat.

St. Lucy is often pictured with a plate bearing a set of eyes. Some say that her eyes were gouged out during her torture. Others believe that she herself removed her eyes and sent them to her spurned suitor because he so admired them. In both versions of the story, her eyes miraculously grew back. We can regard the symbol of Lucy's eyes in another manner, as further evidence of her insight into the human spirit and her vision for her own salvation.

If the eyes are indeed the gateway to the soul, then St. Lucy is eager to provide us with more than a fleeting glimpse into hers. We see a young woman whose faith and strength never wavered. She was not oblivious to the easy life she could have enjoyed if she had denounced her faith. Undoubtedly she saw the dangers in rejecting a powerful suitor and subjecting herself to the mercy of a pagan court. Yet her eyes looked beyond her life here on earth, and her faith bolstered her courage to stand up for her beliefs.

There is so much we parents can learn from Lucy's life, and there are so many ways we can ask her for help as we grapple with our children:

With her help, we can learn to trust our own eyes. When we sense that our child is in trouble, the temptation is to ignore the problem, hoping it will go away. St. Lucy reminds us that seeing is believing. If we see the signs of drug abuse—mood swings, lethargy, failure in school, anger, red eyes, missing money—then we must have faith in our instincts.

St. Lucy can remind us to look into a child's eyes. A high school teacher told a parent assembly that when he wants to know whether a child is telling the truth, he looks into his eyes.

The eyes don't lie, he observed. When you question what your child is telling you, have faith that you will see into his soul by looking into his eyes.

We can ask her to help us stand firm through difficult times. The easy way out may not be the best route to follow. It certainly wasn't for Lucy. Confronting a child may disrupt the harmony in our household, strain our relationships, and perhaps even lead to a crisis. We should have faith, however, that if we follow through, the final result will be a good one.

We can ask her to be with our children when we can't be. Lucy's faith in our Lord never wavered. Because of her steadfastness, her name, which means "light," is invoked in times of temptation. During adolescence, our children spend a great deal of time away from us. When they are out of our sight, we can focus on St. Lucy rather than spend anxious moments thinking the worst, praying that she will infuse them with good sense and judgment.

Along the way, if we demonstrate our faith through our behavior and decisions, we may influence those around us to believe also. Lucy made a believer of her mother. We can do likewise with those in our lives.

STEP TWO: SEEK OUT OTHERS WHO ARE FAITHFUL

St. Lucy Filippini, who lived in Italy from 1672 to 1732, was aptly named. Like the earlier St. Lucy, Lucy Filippini had strong religious beliefs and the commitment to take her message to others. Unlike the third-century Lucy, this later saint lived during a time when Catholics were not being persecuted for their beliefs. Lucy Filippini emerged as a pioneer in showing others how to share their religion and faith with a wider audience.

How did she manage this task? She encouraged religious men and women to venture out from the confines of convents and cloisters and mingle with regular people. While this strategy seems obvious today, back in Lucy Filippini's time the church encouraged religious to engage in solitary prayer. Many religious felt that priests, nuns, and monks who prayed silently, fasted, and did constant penance had a better chance of being heard by God. Also, they could avoid being corrupted by the temptations and influences of the outside world.

Lucy Filippini, however, saw the situation differently. How could a religious person save other souls if he didn't talk with those people who were in danger of eternal condemnation? She felt that men and women who had chosen the religious life had nothing to lose and everything to gain by becoming part of the real world.

In his book *Voices of the Saints,* Bert Ghezzi recounts the story of St. Lucy Filippini. "Those who are sheltered in a cloister find less occasion for sin and greater assurance of salvation," she said. "But they lack the opportunity and merit of working directly for the salvation of souls."

An unforeseen by-product of Lucy Filippini's work with religious was that laypeople were encouraged by her philosophy to live disciplined religious lives without abandoning their place within their homes, workplaces, and communities. While this development was a positive one in Lucy Filippini's time, having these additional religious workers has proved to be essential today. With a shortage of men and women entering religious life, many laypeople have filled the gap. You can see evidence of this evolution in your own community. There are sodalities, prayer groups, rosary societies, and other religious organizations that have as their goal carrying God's word to a larger audience. Within your church, you probably have neighbors and friends who serve as eucharistic ministers, deacons, members of the parish council, and teachers for the religious-education program. We have Lucy Filippini to thank for sparking that revolution.

These laypeople and religious groups provide you with an ideal way to recapture your faith. If your dark side has emerged, if you are angry at God for your parenting situation, you may not be in the best frame of mind to discuss your attitude with a priest or a nun. You may be able, however, to start small by attending a parish council meeting, joining a prayer group, or simply talking with a layperson whose faith you admire but whom you would not find intimidating or judgmental. You may not even want to talk with anyone yet but merely spend your time working alongside those whose faith, at this point in time, is stronger than your own. Some of their religious fervor is bound to rub off on you.

Pray to St. Lucy Filippini that she send your way a messenger who will help you begin the process of recovering your faith. After you have prayed to her, open up your heart. You may not anticipate who your messenger will be; perhaps it will be someone totally unexpected. So be receptive to those who talk with you and share their beliefs.

STEP THREE: VIEW YOUR CRISIS AS A TURNING POINT

Sometimes we need to suffer a trauma in order to rediscover who we are, why we are here, and where we are headed. What we may discover is that our faith has not abandoned us but has merely gone into sleep mode, ready to spring to life stronger and more powerful than ever.

Right now your faith is being tested, perhaps as never before. There may be a reason for this trial. Think of another time in your life when you were tested. Remember when your boss asked you to make an important presentation with only three hours to prepare? How about the time you had to plan your child's birthday party, supervise the painter, help organize a hospital fund-raiser, and nurse your father through a difficult illness? What about that outside event (a flood, fuel shortage, or shipping mix-up, for example) that threw your entire life into chaos?

How did you handle those challenges? Did you give up? Or did you work harder, pull yourself together, and wind up in a better place? You never want to repeat the experience, but looking back, you have to admit that the crisis forced you to grow in confidence, knowledge, and ability. Now you have more faith that you could handle a similar challenge if it came your way.

A magnificent quality of the human spirit is that it doesn't quit easily. When we are tested, we fight. We aren't ready to admit defeat without giving the situation our best shot.

Develop the same attitude about your faith. Don't abandon your beliefs without a fight. Ronda De Sola Chervin found herself plunged into darkness after her son, Charles, took his own life, jumping off a bridge in Big Sur, California. In her book *The Kiss from the Cross: Saints for Every Kind of Suffering,* she characterized the suffering she and her husband endured as "unbearable." They prayed, but those prayers "reached out not toward light but, seemingly, catapulted into sheer darkness or backward toward the memory of the God rather than the living God."

In her quest to escape her pain, she came to the realization that there was no way out. "Instead, pain itself was the road into the heart of Christ where the holiness that had always eluded me might be found," she wrote. "And who better to journey with but the saints whose pilgrim-drink was that grail of intense suffering they eagerly sought at the hands of their beloved!" Many saints experienced a crisis of faith at some point during their lives. Rather than shy away from the pain, they embraced it. This stage is the one you probably find yourself in now. Can you find your way through this pain to a rebirth of faith? Many before you have succeeded in this. We can draw inspiration from reviewing how other saints managed to reawaken their spirit.

One such saint is Alphonsus Rodriguez, who was born in Segovia, Spain, in 1533. His life is a testament to everlasting faith, for he suffered unimaginable tragedies and disappointments yet remained loyal to God.

When Alphonsus was fourteen years old, his father died, leaving him to run the family business. At that young age, Alphonsus did not have the necessary experience and skill, and the business failed. He married when he was twenty-six, but his wife died giving birth. Only a few years later, both his mother and child died also, leaving him without the anchor of family.

Amazingly enough, Alphonsus's faith never died, and he recognized his call to the religious life. This path was not an easy one, either, for he was forced to go back to school to complete the education he had left in midstream. Imagine attending school with your child, and you might have some appreciation for the embarrassment Alphonsus might have felt. Still, he persevered and was finally accepted as a lay brother by the Jesuits of Segovia. Even in this limited role, he was able to influence many people and pass along his faith.

St. Alphonsus's words can inspire us in our own trials: "Another exercise is very valuable for the imitation of Christ—

for love of him, taking the sweet for the bitter and the bitter for the sweet."

STEP FOUR: ACCEPT THAT YOU MAY SUFFER ALONE

Parenting an out-of-control or difficult child can be a lonely experience. Single parents who have no one to share the burden with may find the task overwhelming. Even in families where there is a parenting partner, other relatives, supportive friends, and caring professionals, there will be times when you have to handle a crisis on your own, without being able to consult others. When the phone rings in the middle of the night, you have to trust yourself and find the strength to persevere.

During these desolate moments, think of St. Bernadette Soubirous, who lived in Lourdes, France, during the nineteenth century. Outwardly, there was nothing remarkable about Bernadette. She was one of six children born to a poor miller and his wife. One day, when Bernadette was only fourteen, she set out with one of her sisters and a friend to gather wood. While the other two girls went on ahead, Bernadette was distracted by a rustling of trees and bushes. Looking up, she saw a young woman dressed in white standing in front of a grotto, or cave.

Although the young woman said nothing, Bernadette understood she was being invited to pray. Bernadette knelt down, took out her rosary, and began to pray with the lady. At the end of the rosary, the lady disappeared. Bernadette's companions, finding her kneeling and clutching her rosary, made fun of her. Bernadette explained what had happened and asked them not to tell anyone. But her sister told their mother, who, fearing the apparition might have been a lost soul from purgatory, forbade Bernadette to return to the grotto. However, a few days later, her mother relented. Bernadette went back to the grotto and once again saw the young woman in white.

The woman, who would later identify herself to Bernadette as the Immaculate Conception, appeared to the peasant girl eighteen times, from February to April 1858. Although large crowds sometimes accompanied Bernadette, she was the only one to see the vision. Many skeptics were converted, however, when the Virgin Mother created a spring of fresh water where there had never been one before. Even today, this spring continues to gush forth twenty-seven thousand gallons of water each week. It has been credited with having curative powers, and many pilgrims travel long distances to come to Lourdes to be healed.

Bernadette's trials began after the apparitions ended. She endured numerous interrogations by church officials, some of whom doubted her story. Without anyone to back up her story, she was forced to defend herself alone. Neighbors, friends, and complete strangers tormented her with questions, many of them impolite and disrespectful. Others sought her intercession. Bernadette suffered alone, and it became impossible for her to lead a normal life. If Bernadette had lived during our time, her life probably would have provided considerable material for the tabloid newspapers and reality-based TV dramas.

Finally, she entered the convent of the Sisters of Notre Dame of Nevers, where she attempted to live like an ordinary nun. Not wanting to see her experiences commercialized, she refused to participate in the development of Lourdes as an international destination for pilgrims. During our Lady's visitations to Bernadette, she had asked that a church be built on the site. When the basilica was finally completed in 1876, Bernadette did not attend the opening ceremonies. She was only thirty-five when she died, but in her short lifetime she had touched many people. Her name has become synonymous with visions, and her life was immortalized in the Academy Award–winning motion picture *The Song of Bernadette*.

After her experience with Mary, Bernadette compared herself to a broom, something that had been used for a time (by our Lady, no less) and then put aside. Despite the challenges it brought, she welcomed being cast in what has become one of the Catholic Church's most moving dramas. She never questioned our Lady's motives, asked, "Why me?" or tried to manipulate public opinion. Afterward, she was never resentful over the turn her life had taken.

No one knows why Bernadette, and not one of her sisters or friends, was chosen to see our Lady. Similarly, you cannot know why your parenting duties have become so complex while your relatives and friends enjoy their years with their own teenage children. Pray to St. Bernadette to be with you during moments when you feel alone. Ask her to give you the physical and spiritual strength you need to withstand any crisis that comes your way. When you are confronted with someone who brings you bad news about your child, consider how Bernadette must have felt being constantly questioned by those she had assumed were there to help her. Ask her for guidance in handling such situations.

Even Bernadette sought refuge from the storm. Follow her example. When it seems you cannot escape the turmoil in your life, retreat to a place where you can be quiet and pray. You are never truly alone when you invite God, our Lady, and saints like Bernadette into your life. Later in this chapter, we will give you guidance on constructing a place of refuge within your home.

STEP FIVE: REMEMBER THAT NOTHING—NOT EVEN FAITH— CAN BE WON WITHOUT A FIGHT

During moments when parenting an out-of-control child tests our faith, we can turn to St. Catherine of Siena. This saint, who was born in 1347, never gave up on the biggest battle of her life: convincing the pope to move the papacy from Avignon, France, back to Rome. She ultimately succeeded, and her novena is often said to invoke strength and faith in times of strife and trouble.

We need the tenacity of St. Catherine when parenting a difficult adolescent. Our faith may have been shaken by recent events, but with a renewed sense of purpose, we can emerge strengthened in spirit.

From the beginning, Catherine was a fighter. When she was only six years old, she had a vision that featured our Lord sitting with St. Peter, St. Paul, and St. John. From that moment on, she devoted herself to God and promised him she would never marry.

Her parents, however, had other plans. They tried to dislodge their daughter's devotion and get her to change her mind about not marrying. Every day she was subjected to their harassment. Because she loved solitude, they took her private bedchamber away from her. They forced her to cook, clean, and perform every menial task imaginable. She bore all this with stoicism. In the end, her will proved stronger than theirs. Her parents relented and told her she could follow her own course. Catherine began praying, fasting, and doing penance by sleeping on boards rather than a soft bed.

Even though her parents no longer tormented her, Catherine was not at peace. Whether awake or asleep, she was haunted by evil images and tempted by sin. Just when she was near despair, the Lord and his mother appeared to her. The Savior placed a ring upon Catherine's finger that was meant to symbolize her union with him. The ring remained visible only to Catherine, and she drew considerable strength from its presence. Jesus and his mother advised Catherine to come out of her solitude and carry God's word to her neighbors. Her public service included working as a nurse in hospitals, attending to the most gruesome cases, patients whom even other nurses shunned. She also visited sick people outside of hospitals, in their homes and even in prisons.

Despite all her good works, Catherine remained a controversial figure because of her religious fervor. It didn't help that she saw things other people didn't see. Imagine her telling someone about her invisible ring. Who would believe her? Later on, while praying before a crucifix, she received the wounds, known as stigmata, that mimicked those Christ received when he was hung on the cross. Again, the wounds were visible only to Catherine, although others would see them when she died.

Soon Catherine understood what her greatest mission was to be. She was given the task of convincing the pope to return to Rome from Avignon, France. The residence of the pope may seem a trivial matter that should not have engaged the energies of a great saint like Catherine. Yet during the fourteenth century, the pope was not only a religious leader, but also a political one. Historians contend that much of the social unrest, economic dislocation, and political turmoil that Europe experienced during those years can be traced to the fact that for nearly three-fourths of a century, the popes had been living in France, not Italy.

Catherine's efforts to move Pope Gregory XI back to Rome seemed thwarted at every turn. The powerful French cardinals opposed such an action. In the days before high-speed trains, the trip to Avignon from Italy, as well as the smaller trips from one Italian city to another to bolster support for her plan, taxed her physically. Letters were often a poor substitute, taking long to arrive, and Catherine had no way of knowing that her missives had been received. She had to do everything on her own.

She did succeed finally in moving Pope Gregory to Rome. However, soon after her victory, Gregory died. Urban VI was chosen as his successor, but the French defiantly refused to recognize Urban as pope and chose one of their own. Thus began a schism that threatened to tear apart the Catholic Church once again. Catherine's work was not yet done. She became an essential supporter of Urban VI, writing letters to reiterate her support, visiting him to bolster his resolve, encouraging him to remain strong, and advising him to refrain from harshness, which threatened to alienate some of his supporters.

Besides fighting for the true pope, Catherine spent her time dictating letters to historical figures and common people. She also wrote a book under the inspiration of the Holy Spirit. Known as *The Dialogue of St. Catherine,* this tome includes sections where Catherine recorded God's comments to her. For example, Catherine records God's response to her offer to suffer for others: "You asked for suffering, and you asked me to punish you for the sins of others. You were, in effect, asking for love and light and knowledge of the truth. For suffering and sorrow increase in proportion to love: When love grows, so does sorrow."

Chances are that you, unlike Catherine, did not ask God for suffering. Pain has come your way unbidden. Still, you can find comfort in God's words to Catherine. You are suffering because you love your child. Don't lose sight of that love. You may never be able to achieve Catherine's enthusiasm for turmoil, but you can emulate her fighting spirit.

Don't give up—on yourself, your faith, or your child. Think of the overwhelming task Catherine had before her, to move the papacy. Somehow, with God's help and Catherine's intervention, you will be able to move your child, too.

Using the Senses to Recall Your Faith

Do you remember the faith you possessed as a youth? Remember what it felt like to truly believe that God would answer your prayers? Can you recall a time when you were sitting in church, perhaps during the Christmas season, and the sights, sounds, and smells overwhelmed your senses? It's no secret that our eyes, ears, and noses can act as time machines, transporting us, even without our permission, back through the years, causing us to relive a memory, sometimes happy, sometimes painful.

We can use our senses to help us recapture the faith we had as a child. Here are some ways to do that:

Light a candle. A burning candle has come to symbolize many things: joy, love, reverence for all things holy, purity, knowledge, and even sacrifice, since the very act of burning a candle leads to its demise. Candles can remind us of a simpler time, when people depended on them for light, warmth, and safety.

Candles have long occupied a central place in worship in the Catholic Church. During Mass, candles are lit on the altar. Most churches have a designated place where the faithful can make a monetary offering, light a candle, and pray to a specific saint for help. Perhaps the most auspicious use of candles, however, occurs during holy days. During the Christmas season, many homes and churches display an Advent evergreen wreath in which four candles are inserted. Each week of Advent, one candle is lit as a symbol of the coming of the "Light" of the world. The paschal candle, often large and decorated, is lit during the Lenten season to remind us of Christ's sacrifice.

In some places, candles have become part of the legend accompanying a saint. Einsiedeln, in east-central Switzerland, is a favorite destination for pilgrims all over Europe. The city is home to a Benedictine abbey that was built in the tenth century, reportedly on the site where St. Meinrad, a ninth-century martyr, was imprisoned. Rebuilt in the early eighteenth century, the monastery has been hailed as perhaps the largest and best example of Swiss baroque architecture. A major attraction, however, is within the monastery. It is a statue of the Virgin Mother that has been nicknamed the Black Virgin. The wooden statue has been discolored by the untold number of candles that have been burned in front of it throughout the centuries. One can only imagine the number of petitions that have been placed at the foot of the Virgin.

You can employ candles whenever and wherever you like to create for yourself a peaceful mood. But to help you recapture your religious faith, focus on the candles of your childhood religious experience, the small white votives, or novena candles, that give off their own sweet scent without any added perfumes. These candles are available in most department and hardware stores. You may have to travel to a religious supply store, however, to locate the red glass candleholders commonly used in churches.

Before incorporating candles in your home, you might want to visit your local parish at a time when few people will be there, light a candle in front of a favorite saint, close your eyes, and breathe deeply. Focus on your sense of smell. Take in the aroma of the burning candles. Allow your mind to wander on its own, without any direction from you. You might find yourself traveling back to your childhood and remembering other moments in which you knelt before the statue of a saint. Remember what that felt like. Take that feeling with you, and try to experience it again and again throughout the day, perhaps by saying a quiet prayer.

Burn incense. Along with the fragrance of candles, the sweet smell of incense typifies worship in the Catholic Church, particularly on holy days. Incense—grains of resins mixed with spices—is usually sprinkled on lighted charcoal housed in an ornamental container suspended on a chain. At one point during the Mass, the priest may swing the container while walking around the altar or facing the congregation. The intent is to purify the air, making the atmosphere more pleasing to God.

The use of incense predates the Catholic Church. Ancient cultures, including the Egyptians, the Babylonians, the Hindus, and the Jews, often employed it in their religious rituals. The early Christian church began to use incense in the fourth century. The fragrant smoke came to symbolize the ascent of the prayers of the faithful and the merits of the saints.

Incense was treasured as a precious substance. Frankincense and myrrh, used as incense, were presented to the Christ child as gifts from the three kings. In the seventeenth and eighteenth centuries, people sought out less-expensive ingredients, such as those used in perfume. This trend toward synthetic substitutes continues today.

Attend a High Mass at your local parish. You don't have to sit up front; your olfactory nerves will be able to detect the incense wherever you sit. You won't have solitude, because the incense demands accompaniments—chanting, organ music, the rustling of religious garments—to have an effect. You may find yourself transported back to an occasion long forgotten: a holiday Mass, a christening, a wedding.

Burning incense at home can help you continue any religious experience you had at Mass. Unfortunately, for some people, incense has earned a negative reputation because many teenagers use it to disguise their drug use. On the positive side, because of its popularity, incense is available in many shops and can even be bought on the street in some cities. Find one that is not heavily perfumed. You don't need a fancy container; some incense can be burned in an ashtray or on a small plate.

Play religious music. Christmas is probably the one time when you play religious music in your home. Certainly, well-known carols can reawaken the child in us. Even if we are not feeling religious, it's hard to resist religious sentiment when listening to "Silent Night," "Away in a Manger," "O Little Town of Bethlehem," or "The First Noel."

In the Catholic Church, music is not restricted to Christmastime. All year long, all kinds of music—classical, liturgical, folk—can be heard spilling out of churches nationwide. What type of church music do you remember from your childhood? Do low tones from an organ still vibrate in your soul? Or do you remember someone strumming a guitar and singing "Amazing Grace"? Perhaps traditional hymns like "A Mighty Fortress Is Our God" stir longings for a more peaceful time.

Attend a Mass that features music. Write down the names of songs you remember and would like to listen to again. You can search on the Internet or at a religious bookstore for CDs you can listen to at home.

Celebratory High Masses can easily border on sensory overload; the candles, the incense, the organ music, and the bright liturgical colors create a pageantry that remains unrivaled by other religions. You may be ready to jump back into these rituals in an effort to recapture your faith, but there is something to be said for taking things slow. Select one sense—smell, for example—to test your powers of recall. Attend a quiet Mass that will be sparsely attended, and focus on the tantalizing scent of the candles. The faith you have left behind is there, right under your nose.

BUILD A HOLY PLACE

Some people can worship God wherever they are—on the bus, at the ballpark, in the woods, on the beach. For others, however, it is necessary to seek out a special place to be with the Lord. Such individuals can create a holy place, even a small altar, within their homes where they can pray.

Technically, an altar is a raised structure or place that is used for prayer. When you think of an altar, you probably think of a large stone slab that resembles a long, narrow table. In the Catholic Church, the altar is functional, providing a place where the priest can place the Bible as well as the consecrated bread and wine for communion. A white cloth with a cross in the middle usually covers the altar, and candles are placed at either end. During the Mass, the altar is the focus and represents the presence of Christ during the ceremony.

An altar doesn't have to be a large table-like structure in a church. It can be anything or anywhere, as long as it is used for prayer. For a taxi driver, an altar can be a dashboard upon which a statute of St. Anthony sits, or a rosary hanging from the rearview mirror. In the home, an altar can be the corner of a dresser, part of the fireplace mantel, a small table in the dining room, or a stool placed outside in the rose garden. In different parts of Europe, altars are often constructed in small wooden boxes that look like birdhouses and placed on poles. Inside are various statues and pictures of saints along with offerings—a bottle of olive oil, flowers, a piece of jewelry.

What will your holy place look like? It could simply be a statue of St. Joseph placed on your mantel with a votive candle that can be lit during prayer. You may choose to hang a painting of Mary over your bed and kneel beneath it in the morning, gazing up at her image. The important thing is not what this place looks like, how formal or lavish it is, but whether it can be a place of peace where you can pray and reflect on your faith.

Right now you may feel as if you are in a religious abyss. You probably have never felt so alone, so adrift. Keep in mind that many other people, some of them saints, have shared your journey. They once doubted, but they managed to reawaken their faith. Pray that these saints will show you the way. Open yourself up to whatever you have at your disposal to help you accomplish your goal. Don't doubt your faith. And don't doubt that one day soon you may be able to once again believe in your child.

Prayer to St. Thomas

Dear St. Thomas, on the night our Lord visited the apostles, you were absent. Yet you could not take their word that they had actually seen the risen Christ. Oh, how I share your doubts! You were able to believe only after Jesus himself appeared to you with the physical evidence of his crucifixion. How did you feel when you were finally able to let go of your questions and embrace him with all your heart? I ask that you guide me through these dark days.

Help me find the faith I have lost. Along the way, strengthen my spirit so that one day soon I will be able to spread the word to others. Amen.

Saints Who Can Help You Rekindle Your Faith

St. Lucy can keep you focused on salvation with God.

St. Lucy Filippini can help you find others whose faith is strong.

St. Alphonsus Rodriguez can teach you that faith can survive adversity.

St. Bernadette can walk with you when you are alone.

St. Catherine of Siena can teach you not to give up the good fight.

Discussion Questions

1. St. Lucy wanted to remain a virgin, while her mother, Eutychia, wanted her to marry a rich pagan suitor. Money motivated Eutychia; what motivates you when you set goals for your child? It took a medical miracle to change Eutychia's mind. What would it take for you to embrace even part of your child's dreams?

2. St. Lucy reminds us that the eyes are windows to the soul. When was the last time you really looked into your child's eyes? What did you see? Let your child see your love and concern in your eyes.

3. The ultimate prize, salvation with God, kept Lucy focused on her faith. Can you envision a time when these challenging days with your child will wind down? What will that future look like? How can you draw comfort from the success stories of others?

4. St. Lucy Filippini encouraged religious people to leave the shelter of the cloister and broadcast their beliefs to a wider audience. Are you reluctant to talk about your faith with others? How would doing so benefit you and those around you, particularly your child?

5. "No pain, no gain" is a mantra that helps motivate many athletes. In life, too, growth often comes after a painful experience. Reflect on a trying time from your past. What did you learn during that struggle that might help you now?

6. Parenting a difficult child can be a frightening experience, particularly for a single parent. If you feel alone, examine whether your isolation is self-imposed. Do you lack faith in those around you? How might you go about sharing your burden?

7. St. Catherine's parents opposed her plan never to marry. However, the punishments they doled out failed to shake Catherine's resolve. Are you caught in a similar struggle with your own child? What can you do to break this destructive cycle?

8. Like St. Thomas, we sometimes need tangible proof before we can truly believe. What tangible proof do you need before you can have faith that your child has changed?

9. Having faith means surrendering control. If you lack faith, could your desire for control be holding you back? Think up an activity—riding a roller coaster, being led around blindfolded—that would force you to surrender control to others. From this exercise, can you learn what holds you back from trusting others?

10. Young children must trust adults and so find it easier to give up control and believe. Bring out pictures of yourself as a child, especially ones involving the sacraments, holy days, and other religious events. Try to recapture your childhood faith by reliving those moments.

chapter four

Hope

*Where there is great love,
there are always great miracles.*

—MOTHER TERESA OF CALCUTTA

W hen you have tried everything to help your child and nothing has succeeded, despair descends like a thick, dark fog. Gradually or in an instant, you realize that your dreams for your child—college education, storybook wedding, brilliant career—have been eclipsed by a nightmare. It becomes harder and harder to see any way out. Every day you feel hopelessness sinking in.

When you have lost hope, the only thing to do is turn to God. He is waiting for your call. Take heart from the story of Jesus' death and resurrection. God the Father allowed his only Son to slip into the dark hole of feeling abandoned. Jesus experienced his emotional nadir while nailed to the cross. As recorded in the Gospel according to Mark, Jesus "cried out in a loud voice, 'Eloi, eloi, lama sabachthani?' which means, 'My God, my God, why have you forsaken me?'" (Mark 15:34).

God brought his Son out of the dark and into the light with the Resurrection. God's love is capable of doing the same for you. With God in your sights, nothing—not even your worst catastrophe or heaviest burden—is ever hopeless.

In this chapter, we will show you how to keep hope alive even in circumstances that look hopeless to you. We will offer you a spiritual lifeboat in the stories of the saints, who experienced the intensity of suffering you are experiencing now. In their humanity, they can give you empathy and company; with their sacred deeds, they can give you inspiration.

Not only do you need hope in order to cope with life as you know it, but your child needs it, too, perhaps more than you do. A child who has made a mess of his or her life desperately needs to see hope, not despair, reflected in your eyes. When you are able to rise above your lethargy and gloom and display hope, you set a powerful example for your child to hold on to and follow.

St. Rita of Cascia: Praying through One Crisis at a Time

Feast Day: May 22

St. Rita of Cascia had every right to wallow in despondency. She was trapped in a miserable life full of countless hard times and disappointments.

Rita's life began auspiciously in 1386. While her mother was pregnant with her, an angel visited. The heavenly messenger whispered to her that the baby's name should be Rita—a miraculous sign, but as far as the expectant parents were concerned, this baby was already a miracle. An older couple who owned a farm in Italy, they had waited a long time before being blessed with a child.

Like many parents, they wanted only the best for their beloved child. Like countless mothers and fathers, they were convinced they knew exactly what that meant: marriage. Rita's own life plan couldn't have been more different. Since as far back as she could remember, the only union that she dreamed of was with God. She wanted to enter the convent.

Putting aside her own desires, Rita obeyed her parents. At the age of twelve, she surrendered to an arranged marriage with Paul di Ferdinando. Unfortunately, her parent's choice of husband proved dismal. Life with Paul was sheer misery for Rita. He became a local gangster, a well-known womanizer, and an abusive husband. Rita stayed with him and bore him two sons. She endured public humiliation and private abuse. One can only imagine the embarrassment and terror that she must have lived with every day not knowing where her husband was, whom he was with, or when he would turn vicious.

What sustained Rita? Prayer. Not only did prayer get her through her days, but it also rescued her from becoming bitter and hopeless. One day, eighteen years into the marriage, Rita's brutal and selfish husband had an epiphany. Paul realized how horrible a husband he had been and expressed his sincere remorse to his loyal wife. It sounded like answered prayers, but the happily-ever-after scenario still eluded Rita. As fate would have it, the only truth to their marriage vow turned out to be "till death do us part." A few short weeks after Paul's apology, Rita found his mutilated body on her doorstep. Apparently he had been murdered, the victim of a vendetta.

Rita's two sons vowed to avenge their father's death. In their character Rita saw the same violent ways and values of their father. She prayed to God to prevent them from carrying out their vindictive plan. She couldn't bear the thought of her boys becoming murderers. Again, her prayers were answered, although she still suffered greatly: both of her sons fell ill and died, but not before making peace with their mother.

When Rita buried her sons she was thirty years old, child-less, and a widow. Yet she wasn't angry with God for her lot in life or for the way he responded to her prayers. In fact, Rita accepted God's will and her fate, seeing it as an opportunity to finally enter religious life, her original plan.

She applied to the local Augustinian convent but was met with rejection time and again. The reason the convent gave her was that she was no longer a virgin. Once again, Rita relied on prayer and refused to give up. She directed her spiritual conver-sations to three favorite saints: St. John the Baptist, St. Nicholas of Tolentino (a thirteenth-century friar known for his street-corner preaching and peacemaking ability), and St. Augustine. According to legend, Rita was transported miraculously into the midst of the cloister. Realizing that this woman was special, the convent reversed its objections and accepted her.

Rita flourished in her vocation, caring for the older sickly nuns. It appeared that when Rita prayed, the impossible often happened, as with her prodigal husband and her miraculous entry into the convent. Her illness and death were also marked by answered prayers.

One of Rita's favorite meditations was Christ's crucifixion and death, especially his crown of thorns. As Rita begged to feel a part of that suffering, a thorn became fixed to her own fore-head. The wound festered, causing a persistent infection and a strong unpleasant smell. Rita lived an isolated existence for the next fifteen years, until she died of tuberculosis in 1457. On the day she died, her body took on the delicious fragrance of roses as these flowers bloomed outside, quite out of season. The aroma wafted throughout the convent, and it still does to this day. Rita's body is enshrined there in glass, and over the years her shrine at Cascia has become the site of many miracles. Consequently, St. Rita of Cascia is often called the saint of impossible causes.

Rita endured dashed dreams, deep disappointments, the death of her husband and both her sons, and sickness. Yet she never wallowed in hopelessness. She believed in the power of prayer and trusted in God. She relied on her rapport with her favorite saints to keep her from despair. Modeling her behavior can help you, too.

REACH OUT TO PRAYER

Hopelessness is like a tunnel or a black hole: you get sucked into it. You feel alone and abandoned. When you are trapped like this and floundering alone, there is a concrete way to get your spiritual footing. Hold on to the power of prayer. Reach out to a saint. Saints like St. Rita know intimately your pain and distress. Furthermore, they know your potential, and your child's, and they can help you if you trust them to do so.

"The saints themselves expected to be doing the work of intercession once they got to heaven," says Bert Ghezzi, author of *Voices of the Saints*. "The church gives us saints as intercessors and as patrons. We are encouraged to ask the saints to pray with us and to invite them to protect and guide us on our journey."

There are many ways to pray: silently, formally, communally, or individually. One form of prayer in particular, though, is perfectly suited to hopelessness. This prayer type, called the novena, is petitionary, or intercessory, because it involves asking for a specific request. Novenas are usually said when one is in an impossible predicament and in need of a miracle. Like a protocol of treatments and medicines prescribed to cure a disease, or a series of exercises suggested to restore harmony to a troubled relationship, the novena can be a spiritual tool to rid you of despair.

The novena combines formal prayers and the pray-er's own personal entreaty. Novenas start with specific prayers to God, the Virgin Mother, or a special saint. Somewhere in the prayer you are asked to fill in your own personal request. The prayers of a novena are repeated for nine days in a row. When you make a novena, the purpose is to ask the heavenly listener to grant you your special request, called your "intention." With a novena you telegraph your real-life melodrama and implore God, the Blessed Mother, or a particular saint to help you. If you decide to address a special saint, the ideal novena would begin nine days prior to the chosen saint's feast day.

The first novena dates back to the time of Christ and his apostles. According to Scripture, before Christ ascended to heaven after his resurrection, he told the apostles to spend nine days praying for guidance. They obeyed Jesus' instructions, and the Holy Spirit appeared to them, taking on the form of a burning tongue. Each apostle suddenly had the gift of knowing many languages and the ambition to spread the word of God. During the Middle Ages, a special novena to the Holy Spirit was written to commemorate this event.

Over the years, many different novenas have been written. In addition to invoking help from God or the Virgin Mary, people began praying to the patron saints and asking them to intercede with God. Why were these holy men and women elected? The saints were first and foremost human beings with the capacity to understand the heavy burdens and problems we encounter. Many saints, like St. Rita, had personal knowledge of what human beings go through. Bad marriages, dysfunctional families, episodes of reckless living—for every situation there is a saint who, as they say, has "been there, done that." Because the saints achieved a level of sanctity, their relics revered over the years, they were also invested with spiritual power. Many were known as divine healers and were capable of granting favors, even miracles.

Novenas are often printed in pamphlets that can be found at your local parish. Or you might ask your parents or older relatives if they have favorite novenas that they have recited in times of strife. There is something especially reassuring about a novena that has been passed from one generation to the next. If no one in your family is familiar with this form of prayer, you can also locate novenas in various book collections. Three recent ones containing many devotions to saints are *Mention Your Request Here: The Church's Most Powerful Novenas,* by Michael Dubruiel; *Treasury of Novenas,* by Lawrence G. Lovasik; and *Novena: The Power of Prayer,* by Barbara Calamari and Sandra DiPasqua.

The novena is a resource that Jesus himself introduced and is waiting for you to tap into. It can be your saving grace when you can't figure out how to survive or what to do.

How to Cast Your Intention

When you are faced with a sudden trauma or an ongoing battle with a difficult child, it's natural to want to wish it away. If only you could say a bedtime prayer, go to sleep, and awaken the next day to a "cured" child. If only your child's legal battles or pregnancy or illness would vanish. Your first instinct is to pray for a miracle and hope for an instantaneous resolution.

While miracles do happen, they rarely occur overnight. Nor are they likely to materialize in the nine-day span of the typical novena. If your adolescent is addicted to drugs or alcohol, he probably won't walk out of his bedroom one morning recovered. The pregnant teen and the father of the child cannot instantly undo the act of creating a life. Even if they choose abortion, which goes against the church's teaching about the sacred value of life, the consequences linger. Your chronically depressed or ill teenager probably won't awaken on the tenth day joyfully singing and dancing around your house.

Rather than casting your intention as a plea for an instant resolution, pray that you and your child will find a way to cope with, conquer, or learn from this crisis. A novena allows you to move forward one prayer at a time. *Novena* coauthors Barbara Calamari and Sandra DiPasqua note that "not only is it [making a novena] a spiritual sacrifice, but it is also a way to allow the subconscious to face a real problem and to consider solutions for it." In other words, repeating the novena is a spiritual opportunity as well as a physical task. It gives you something concrete to do to distance yourself from despair. It helps you find direction and focus at a time when you can't think positively at all. It can even show you the meaning of your struggle.

In order to give you more practice in structuring your intention, we are going to introduce you to several saints whose lives happened to be steeped in typical dilemmas faced by parents with troubled adolescents. We are including their feast days in case you want to plan your novena around them. However, it's not necessary to do that if you want to get started immediately. As you read the lives of these saints, you will surely find one to whom you can relate.

St. John Bosco: A Saint for Out-of-Control Teenagers

Feast Day: January 31

A parent sent us the following plea:

Help! The other evening my sixteen-year-old daughter and a couple of boys and girls went out to shoot a video for a school project. I just happened to look at the tape that she left in the camera the next day. I was appalled at the language, but it was the content that stopped me dead in my tracks. The filming showed my teen and others playing practical and highly dangerous jokes on drivers of automobiles. If that wasn't hair-raising enough, the film showed them shooting out streetlights with a pellet gun. These teens my daughter is running with have me worried sick. I just know that they spell trouble. How do I rescue her before she becomes a lawless juvenile delinquent?

This parent stumbled upon the evidence early on that her child had embarked on a dangerous road with a bunch of risky companions. Many parents have the same sinking feeling about their teens but do not trust their intuition. They get that call from the police station in the midnight hours. The charges vary: assault, arson, robbery, rape.

In our book *Parenting 911,* we report that juveniles accounted for 12 percent of all violent crimes—8 percent of murders, 12 percent of forcible rapes, 17 percent of robberies, and 12 percent of aggravated assaults—according to the Justice Department's Office of Juvenile Justice and Delinquency Prevention statistics for 1997. Arrests of young people under fifteen years old rose 94 percent between 1980 and 1995.

Increasingly, our society's reaction to these teens-gone-wrong smacks of despair. A September 2000 *New York Times* exposé chronicled how too many hapless teenagers who get involved in fights, theft, or arson are sentenced as adults and sent to adult penitentiaries. In such places, an education in crime, not rehabilitation, is the more common result. It's as if we as a society have decided that troubled teens are a hopeless lot.

Don't buy into that pessimism. Don't give up on your child. If you find your teenager is skirting delinquency or in its grips, turn to St. John Bosco. John Bosco was a contemporary of Charles Dickens, but while Dickens wrote about the hard knocks of life and how children are lured into crime in classics like *Oliver Twist,* John Bosco devoted his life to turning around such neglected, exploited, and seemingly expendable boys and girls.

At the tender age of nine, John had a dream that revealed to him what his life's work would be. In that dream, John saw himself surrounded by screaming and out-of-control children. He tried soothing them with words. When that strategy failed, John tried restraining a few physically and threatened to beat them if they didn't settle down. A woman appeared. She suggested that John lead them with a shepherd's staff into a pasture. Once there, the blustering brood turned into wild animals and then into gentle lambs. John awoke knowing his calling: to help struggling children find better lives.

Afterward John became a street entertainer, a pied piper who attracted young boys on Sunday mornings with his juggling, acrobatics, and magic tricks. Once he had their attention, he encouraged them to attend Mass. As a teenager, John entered the seminary but continued his Sunday showcase, which had attracted a local following. He soon decided he wanted to do more for these boys. Along with his mother as housekeeper, John opened a refuge for homeless boys in a suburb of Turin, Italy. He not only provided food, shelter, and clothing but also taught them trade skills like shoemaking and tailoring and set up a printing press. And he continued with his recreational nurturing. By the 1850s John had ten priests helping him with the shelter. He turned his staff into the Salesian order, named after one of his favorite saints, St. Francis de Sales.

Boys weren't the only ones he tried to salvage emotionally and spiritually. In 1859, he organized Daughters of Our Lady, Help of Christians, under the leadership of St. Mary Mazzarello to care for girls and build similar programs for them.

It wasn't always easy for John to turn his dream of rescuing adolescents into a reality. Along the way he butted heads with corrupt clergy who tried to stop his efforts and with anticlerical foes as well. He trusted God to help him when the going got rough. Miracles did happen. On one occasion when food was insufficient, it multiplied just like the famous loaves and fishes in the Bible. Oftentimes, dreams showed John how to reach or know one of his more challenging children. With a combination of trust in God and loving faith in his charges, John flourished in his vocation—and many boys and girls flourished, too. At the end of his days, John Bosco had seen 768 members enter his Salesian order and the houses increase to 38 in Europe and 26 throughout the rest of the Western Hemisphere.

St. John had a gift for handling and guiding adolescents. His affinity was reputed to be part inborn and part experiential. Once he wrote that he did not recall ever having to formally punish a boy—a remarkable fact, considering that his charges were what we would call juvenile delinquents. He relied on making studies and chores fun and used preventive tactics rather than repressive ones.

Because of his commitment and nurturing ability, St. John Bosco is the perfect saint to consult about your own troubled child. Rather than pray for him to transform your teen overnight, cast your intention like this:

- Help me find the words to talk to my child so he will listen to me and talk to me again.

- Show me how to lead my child toward productive activities that he can do well and enjoys doing.

- Let me understand what we are both supposed to learn from this detour.

A novena to St. John Bosco should be cast as a prayer not just for your child but also for yourself. Let John inspire you to become more like he was, more skilled at guiding your child until he is once again on the right road.

St. Dymphna: A Saint Who Lived alongside Mental Illness

Feast Day: May 15

A great number of adolescents suffer from clinical depression and other mental illnesses, according to the National Mental Health Association. If your child suffers from a mental illness, you may sympathize with this mother on the verge of despair:

> My daughter is almost fourteen. She lies constantly and then is obsessed with confessing. She is depressed. She hasn't a single friend at school because she's always doing the wrong thing. We are seeing a child psychologist who has put my daughter on antidepressants. Yesterday's appointment with him left me feeling so hopeless. Before going, I felt maybe he would have an answer to explain why my daughter acts this way or directions on what we can do to fix her. I almost hoped she had ADD or something that we would be able to treat so she would snap out of this.

We've met a steady stream of parents with stories about teenage sons and daughters who struggle with many different mental illnesses: phobias, eating disorders, bipolar disorders, obsessive-compulsive behaviors, and the rages and melancholy of depression. One mother of a fifteen-year-old son became alarmed by her son's behavior:

> *In the last six months my son has turned into a shower freak. He takes a shower in the morning, sometimes a shower in the afternoon after getting home from school, and/or another shower at night. He says he "feels bad," and the shower helps. He has severe mood swings and gets argumentative. My husband says he'll grow out of this.*

Fortunately, many forms of mental illness are discussed openly now. TV programs, Web sites, and magazine articles have put faces on a variety of conditions. So putting two and two together isn't as hard for parents as it used to be when it comes to psychological and emotional syndromes.

When you find out that something is really wrong with your child, and what the name of that something is, it is only the beginning. There is no snapping out of such conditions. A teen who has depression, anxiety, phobias, or compulsions is usually on a long, bumpy road of treatment, which can include experimenting with new and different medications as well as attending therapy. As if all this trial and error with antidepressants and going from specialist to psychiatrist to therapist isn't hard enough, there is the day-to-day reality of mood swings with which a parent must contend. When your child is angry and hostile, morose and withdrawn, or extraordinarily fearful, it makes your life extremely stressful. You know what we are talking about. Even perfect parents, if such a species existed, would crack under the strain.

To make matters more draining, many parents whose children suffer mental maladies find themselves simultaneously struggling with similar afflictions. Mental illnesses run in families. Fighting off their own phobia or melancholy, these parents often say they don't know if they have the innerstrength and resources to manage their adolescent's mental burdens, too.

Dusting off that old platitude "God doesn't give you anything you can't handle" doesn't make coping easier; in fact, it can make you feel more incompetent. Rather than chastising yourself in this way, meet a saint who understands.

Born in 605 in Ireland, Dymphna was fourteen when her mother died. Dealing with her sadness was just the beginning of a terrible aftermath. Her mother had been a devout Christian and had raised Dymphna accordingly. Her dad, Damon, on the other hand, didn't embrace Christianity. Even though he was a powerful king in Ireland, Damon was powerless in the face of death. His grief overwhelmed him. Perhaps having spiritual resources would have helped, or perhaps faith couldn't have altered his genetic makeup. The trauma drove him to bizarre behavior. Damon ordered underlings to scour his territory for a woman who physically resembled his deceased queen. He planned to marry any look-alike, but no such woman could be located.

Dymphna was the one female who looked just like her mother, more each day. Damon became fixated with the idea of marrying his daughter. In his unstable state of mind, the fact that this would be incest did not register. The details are sketchy, but it is believed that Dymphna's father also sexually abused her. So Dymphna ran away. She fled from him and this abominable sin, first abroad to Antwerp and finally to Gheel.

Her father searched for a year until he located her. When he demanded that she return, Dymphna refused, so he killed her with his sword. Dymphna was buried there on the spot.

In those days, people who suffered from epilepsy or dementia were pariahs without homes. Five such homeless and ill people fell asleep at Dymphna's grave site and were miraculously cured. Around the thirteenth century, a brick with her name engraved on it was found near her grave. Again, mentally ill sufferers who visited her tomb experienced miraculous healings. Eventually, a hospital was built in Gheel dedicated to treating those afflicted with nerves, now called anxiety, and other disorders.

Pray to St. Dymphna. As a teenage girl she had to cope with the death of her mother and the loss of her father to his delusional behavior. She had to endure his rages and abuse in addition to her own sadness and terrors. Dymphna had to flee and leave behind everything familiar and live with a paranoid fear of being found. She intimately knows how hard it is to have melancholy, rages, and irrational behavior in the home. You can always pray to her for a miraculous healing, but also cast your intention in this way:

- Grant me stability and an even temper so I can deal with my child's ups and downs.

- Keep me from getting swept up in my child's anger and striking back. Protect me from becoming immobilized by my child's depression.

- Help me get past the everyday dramas and think clearly so I can evaluate which protocols are helpful to my child and which ones have harmful side effects.

A novena to St. Dymphna can help you tackle every day in a way that models optimism and joy for the little things. Dymphna had God. You have them both.

Venerable Matt Talbot:
An Almost-Saint
Who Knows Addiction

Feast Day: June 7

Unlike heroin, cocaine, alcohol, and cigarettes, marijuana and designer drugs like Ecstasy are not addictive, at least not physiologically. They do not cause one's body to crave the substance. That point sounds like quibbling if you are the parent of an adolescent who is using marijuana. A drug habit does damage, whether physically or emotionally. The substance becomes the center of your teen's thoughts and actions. Planning to get high, getting high, finding the substance to get high again—substance abuse is a vicious and monopolizing cycle. The effects of drug abuse, from euphoria to agitation and withdrawal, destroy all semblance of a normal life for an adolescent and the family torn apart by trying to change the behavior. Scolding, grounding, pleading—all fall on deaf ears with a teenager who is lost and only thinking about when and how he can get stoned.

A child may feel bad for any number of reasons, and there is one sure way to feel better, which is why young people continue to take drugs or abuse alcohol. A drink washes away those negative feelings; a toke blows them up in smoke. So it is difficult for a child to break the cycle of substance abuse.

Watching your child become enslaved to alcohol, cocaine, or marijuana is a recipe for hopelessness. Even more heart-wrenching is watching a teenager in rehab relapse. You look ahead to the future, and all you see is your child still struggling with hard or soft drugs or the demon rum. You contemplate the poor odds for beating this problem and the relapses that are considered part of the disease. What kind of a future is this for your son or daughter? It seems like an overwhelmingly depressing one, and that can leave you in despair.

If you are a recovering alcoholic or substance abuser yourself, you feel worse. You know the weight of addiction. You may feel guilty because you passed along to your child a genetic predisposition. When addiction seems too powerful to face, it is time to sit down with Venerable Matt Talbot.

You may not find him in many books detailing the lives of saints because he is a saint in the making. Becoming a saint is a process. The earliest saints recognized by the church were men, women, and children martyred for their faith. Around the fourth century, when widespread persecutions stopped, sainthood was determined by different criteria, based on life—an exemplary one—and not death.

Today, the process of naming someone a saint involves a number of steps. The Congregation for the Causes of Saints, a sainthood review board, thoroughly examines the person's life. At different stages of the review process, the person is given different titles. The title of "Venerable" is bestowed on martyrs and those who displayed virtue in an outstanding manner. When it has been determined that the person attained a state of blessedness in his or her life, the person is beatified, or given the title of "Blessed," and the pope authorizes limited veneration within a country or religious order. Canonization is the pinnacle. At that point the pope allows the saint to be venerated universally. A saint's feast day is the day he or she died, commemorating the person's entry into heaven.

Venerable Matt is on his journey toward sainthood, still subject to the judgment of others. Even though he is not an official saint, you can pray to him for guidance if your child is struggling with addiction. There are saints who are considered the patron saints of substance abusers and alcoholics, such as St. Matthias—an apostle who was beheaded on the shores of the Caspian Sea—but Venerable Matt may be a more empathetic choice. While Matthias is the patron saint of drunkards, he wasn't afflicted with alcoholism. Venerable Matt, on the other hand, was.

Matt Talbot was born in the mid-nineteenth century. His father was an alcoholic, and Matt probably carried the genetic flaw that made him vulnerable to alcoholism. His first taste of alcohol changed his young life. He was twelve, and he was working his first job, at a wine-bottling store in Dublin, Ireland. He tasted the wine, tasted some more, and went home drunk. Rarely, despite his parents' efforts to punish him, was he sober after that first binge.

After sixteen years of abusing alcohol, twenty-eight-year-old Matt hunted down a priest and made a pledge not to drink for three months. When he succeeded in staving off his addiction for those three months, he made another pledge and another, a little longer each time. One day, he vowed not to take a drink ever again for the rest of his life.

Like many recovering alcoholics and substance abusers, Matt took precautions to avoid temptation. One of his strategies was never to carry money. After his conversion, the desire to relapse became too strong; if he didn't have any money, then he couldn't stop into a tavern and buy a drink. He soon discovered that his plan was not a surefire one. Once, without a penny in his pocket, he went into a pub and tried to buy a drink. No one would serve him. Still thirsting, Matt went to a church and stayed there until it closed.

We don't know all that much about the following years of Matt's life: he worked hard, spent a great deal of time in prayer and penance, and donated most of his earnings to charity. In 1891, he joined the Franciscan Third order and found community support. In 1925, at the age of sixty-nine, Matt Talbot died on the way to Mass. Heart failure was the cause. He had been faithful to his pledge for forty-one years.

Forty-one years is a long time to remain sober. Even when you think of it as "one day at a time," the way recovering alcoholics do, the urge to drink remains. Matt undoubtedly prayed for strength and fortitude on many a night. Surely God helped him resist a compelling—and even physically programmed—need to drink.

Matt wasted his entire youth, from twelve to twenty-eight, self-destructing. Probably during those years he tried to quit cold turkey but relapsed again and again. Not until he turned to God in heaven did he find the inner resources to turn his life around and stay sober.

If your family is struggling with substance abuse, say a novena to this saint in the making. Cast your intention to Venerable Matt in this way:

- Accept the weakness in all of us. It is in living with our weaknesses that we can learn to show strength.

- Support my child until she becomes substance free, even if I don't understand this problem.

- Show me how to cultivate fortitude in myself and in my teenager when he relapses. Give me the words of wisdom to help him try again.

- Protect my child from the harmful acquaintances that encourage his substance abuse. Lead him instead toward those who can help him help himself.

The story of this holy man and his addiction is a lesson in and testimony to the power of prayer. God is listening, and so is Venerable Matt.

St. Anne: Coping with a Pregnant Teenager

Feast Day: July 26

Discussing sex with young adolescents is awkward. No one jumps at the chance to discuss sexual intercourse or oral sex with an eleven-year-old boy or a thirteen-year-old girl. It's not unusual for parents to postpone such conversations because they are so uncomfortable. You've tried to explain modesty to your teenage daughter. She just doesn't get the concept. How could she when pop stars and actors pride themselves on looking as bare as possible? Girls aren't the only ones affected by the youth culture; boys bare their bodies, too.

Talking about sex and modesty with adolescents seems like a waste of time. Little by little you slip into denial, even when you intuit signs of your son's or daughter's experimenting with sex. Then one day you get the news—a baby is on the way. Maybe on some level you are not surprised at all. Or maybe you never even saw the two of them together.

Either way, you know what these parents are going through:

We just found out our son is going to be a father at seventeen! He and his girlfriend (sixteen) are keeping the baby and raising him or her themselves. Are these two crazy? They don't work. They don't drive. They have not a clue about what goes into parenting, but they do have attitudes! Last night when we asked how things were going, our son indignantly responded, "Don't worry about it. It isn't your problem anyway! It's OUR decision." Yeah—HIS decision and OUR responsibility.

I don't want to be a grandma! I'm only forty! How long do you "support" people who make poor decisions? How many children of couples like this turn out okay? My husband and I both work. We have bills to pay. Quite honestly, I don't know if I can help raise an infant. That's why we opted for an only child ourselves. I know they'll depend on us for rides, money, babysitting, and all the other "joys" of grandparenting. What if she decides in future months or years to cut him out and us, too? Then we have to deal with that anguish. My fifty-year-old husband is having chest pains over this whole thing! We're disgusted with our son's attitude, sad about the circumstances, feeling guilty, and just plain out of hope.

Becoming a grandparent was supposed to be one of the most wonderful moments in your life, and it wasn't supposed to happen for years. Now that it is happening in your child's middle or high school years, it's anything but wonderful. You don't want to celebrate this new life. You want things to go back to the way they were before you heard the news. You know a baby changes one's life forever. Your child doesn't know this. Who is going to care for this new life? Your son is still a child himself. Your daughter needs her education. You know that, for you, abortion is out of the question. What are you—what is she, what is he—going to do?

When you have no idea how you will be able to face this, think of St. Anne, the mother of the Virgin Mary.

Despite her status as the grandmother of Jesus, little is known about Mary's mother and Joseph's mother-in-law. In Brittany, it was traditionally believed that Anne was a princess. The legend goes that she was whisked away from her homeland aboard a ship of light with an angel as its pilot and taken to Judea. Anne married a man named Joachim, who is also little known. After twenty years of marriage, God had not yet blessed the couple with a child. During the time in which Anne lived, being infertile brought great shame. Neighbors shunned the couple. Rumor had it that they must be cursed.

When Anne gave birth to Mary, it looked as if all their prayers had worked. The Gospels do not offer stories about the kind of child little Mary was, but it's well known that she became pregnant before marriage. Can you imagine what Anne thought when her daughter told her that she was with child? Furthermore, what was her reaction when Mary explained the circumstances of her "immaculate conception"? Mary planned to marry Joseph, but she told Anne that the child was not his. She told her mother about the angel appearing to her, about this child being God's only Son. What went through Anne's mind when she heard these things?

We know only that Anne accepted Mary's explanation with faith and courage. It still couldn't have been easy. Direct your novena to her. Cast your intention in this way:

- Help me appreciate new life as always a sacred blessing—a beginning, not an end.

- Give me the strength to offer the support my child and grandchild will need.

- Show me where to find the financial resources, the energy, and the time to help my child become the parent he or she needs to become.

- Let my child contemplate the alternative, if necessary: an adoption plan so the baby will have loving and caring parents. Inspire my child to be able to adjust to that sacrifice.

Anne has been where you are now. She knows exactly the kind of qualities and insights you need.

St. Jude: The Saint of Impossible Causes

Feast Day: October 28

Chronic illness or a disability isn't a child's fault. Yet that child—and you, the parent—has to deal with the situation. Sometimes life just isn't fair. Read what this mother has to say:

My son is having such a hard time. He is twelve and will be starting eighth grade at a new charter school in September. He had a stroke seven years ago after heart surgery. That affects him physically. He can't use his left hand and has a limp and poor balance. It affects him even more emotionally. He has outbursts of anger and is very impulsive. He is different from other kids and doesn't have any close friends. That in itself breaks my heart. To complicate matters, his older brother is healthy and popular, has wonderful friends, and is always doing

something. Justin feels so left out and jealous. He is con-
stantly depending on ME for his entertainment, and
frankly, I don't have enough money to do all he wants—
from movies to outings to video games—to make him
happy! He can't do the usual things kids do to make
extra money because of his physical limits. I can't make
other kids want to hang out with him. I can't be his 24/7
playmate. I don't know how to help him. I am at the end
of my rope with exhaustion and out of ideas.

You may be the parent of a child who is in even worse circumstances. He survived an automobile accident but was left
paralyzed. She was the victim of a school shooting, left emotionally traumatized and physically impaired. He has AIDS.
With some fates, there is no adapting, only accepting. This can
be the most hopeless scenario of all.

Like St. Rita, St. Jude specializes in impossible causes. Jude
was one of the original twelve apostles. It is believed that after
Jesus' resurrection and ascension into heaven, Jude went to
Mesopotamia to preach the gospel. A legendary competition
with pagan sorcerers and magicians ensued. On one occasion
the local sorcerers struck all the lawyers in the community
dumb. Jude held up a crucifix before the silenced lot, and their
speech returned. In another tale, Jude sent serpents to bite some
wicked magicians but then ordered the serpents to suck out the
venom so that his adversaries recovered. Aside from these
exploits, Jude cured leprosy and performed other impressive
miracles against great odds, making him a powerful figure of
authority. Despite his demonstrated powers, however, Jude met
the fate of many of his Christian contemporaries. He was
stoned to death for his beliefs.

Down through the ages, in spite of his exploits and miracles,
Jude was not a popular saint. Because his name resembled that

of Judas Iscariot, he was often confused with the infamous apostle who betrayed Jesus Christ with a kiss. Folklore implied that Jude was not prayed to as frequently as others and therefore had the time to concentrate on those in desperate circumstances. His reputation grew as the patron saint of impossible causes.

If you pray to St. Jude, there is one string attached. When your request is granted, you must publicly thank him.

When you think no one can grant you the miracle you desire, make your novena to St. Jude. Cast your intention in this way:

- Get my child to the specialists who can be most helpful and most compassionate.

- Show me how to find meaning and joy in every day with my child.

- Steer my child to skills and activities that will help him feel productive and fulfilled.

- Help me trust in God's will, even when there is the possibility that my child might die.

When your hopelessness threatens to overtake you, hang on to the lifeboat of trust. God has created in his image many men and women who have walked that proverbial mile in your shoes. Pray to them. Know that they are there to hear your prayers and intercede with God on your behalf. The novena is the devotion that was created exactly for the despair you are feeling.

Locate a novena to your chosen saint. Schedule the brief time needed to say the novena at the same time each day for nine days. Saying it at the same time every day—whether first thing in the morning or right before you go to sleep—will make you less likely to forget it. If, however, you do miss a day, don't panic. The novena's success is not undermined if you are not perfect. Just make up the day. With the door to novenas always open, the door to help is never closed.

In the end, when you and those most precious to you are gripped in seemingly hopeless situations, you must turn to Jesus. He is always there to rescue you from the worst. All you have to do is ask for his help.

Prayer for Hope

Dear God, I am so low that I can hardly bear to open myself up to anyone, even you. My child may not be innocent, but she [he] is too young to face this disgrace and ruin, this hardship and failure. When I see the troubles that have been visited upon me and my family, it's hard for me to believe that a kind and benevolent God exists. Still, I am making this leap of faith to trust in you. I am going to put one foot in front of the other and confide in saints like St. Rita and St. Jude, who have shown me the power of prayer and the possibility of miracles. This hopelessness is immobilizing me, so I am going to rely on one saint who can help me find meaning in these burdens I carry. Venerable Matt knew addiction, and St. John Bosco saw through delinquency to the heart of troubled adolescents. St. Anne handled her child's pregnancy, and St. Dymphna intimately knew the torment of mental illness. These stories restore my hope. I turn to you and to these saints to help me take baby steps and guide me until I can find my own way out of this darkness. When I feel most alone, I will remind myself that I am not alone. You are there to wipe my tears, show me meaning, and deliver me to love. Forever and ever, amen.

Saints Who Can Rekindle Hope

St. Rita can center you when nothing is going your way.

St. John Bosco can be a role model of restraint and optimism when your teen is out of control.

St. Dymphna can console you when you and your teen are fighting depression.

Venerable Matt Talbot can keep you grounded if your child is held hostage by drugs or alcohol.

St. Anne can show you that every child is a miracle.

St. Jude can be summoned when parenting seems like a mission impossible.

Discussion Questions

1. Your child's behavior has dashed your hopes. Even though you have caught her in a sexually charged encounter, or caught a whiff of cigarette smoke on her clothing or the waft of beer on her breath, could you be overreacting?

2. Unlike St. Alphonsus, who disobeyed his father and refused to marry, St. Rita obeyed her parents and married. In the end, both reached sainthood. What does this say about obedience with regard to children?

3. St. John Bosco's dreams foretold his destiny to turn around delinquents. Screaming children invaded his slumber, as did a

strange woman telling him to shepherd rather than restrain them. Have you had any especially vivid dreams that could be trying to tell you something?

4. When dealing with troubled boys, one of St. John Bosco's most effective tactics turned out to be engaging them in productive activities. Have you tried steering your troubled child into a hobby, an extracurricular activity, or lessons that build on a talent or interest she possesses?

5. Just as Mary confessed an unbelievable story to St. Anne, your child has given you an unbelievable explanation of a crisis. The drugs aren't his; the suspension from school wasn't his fault. You believe he's lying through his teeth. Are you rushing to judgment? Could there be more truth to what you are hearing than you are willing to believe?

6. Recent studies suggest that anxiety and depression stem from the same genetic quirk. Similarly, addictions to alcohol, nicotine, and other substances are linked to body chemistry. If your child is fighting a mental illness or addiction, look beyond his individual struggle and at your family history. Are there lessons to be learned from the family tree, helpers to be tapped into?

7. If you are in a situation that feels hopeless, if you are thinking that life isn't fair, is self-pity getting the best of you? Pessimism can be immobilizing. On the flip side, optimism is a learned behavior. Turn your crisis upside down and see if some unacknowledged opportunity lurks within the situation. Ask yourself: Is this happening to my family for a reason?

8. St. Dymphna suffered the death of her mother and the loss of her father to delusions and irrational behavior. Have you considered that your child's distress could be linked to a loss? The loss of a good friend, innocence, a good reputation? Could his anger or her withdrawal be disguised grief?

9. When St. Jude, the saint of impossible causes, grants you a request, tradition insists you announce a public thank-you. Implied in the St. Jude protocol is gratitude. In the midst of your distressing circumstances, can you find something to be grateful for? Friends, health, other supportive children? Write these down in a "gratitude journal" and return to it when you have more to add or need consolation.

10. Is your praying little more than bargaining ("God, if you do this for me, then I will do that for you")? Rather than giving God orders, can you pray in a language that takes on a more passive quality? What might happen if you become less demanding and more trusting?

chapter five

Patience

O Lord, how long? How long?
Will you be angry forever?
Do not remember our age-old sins.

—ST. AUGUSTINE

Parenting often tries our patience. When we are faced with a daughter who is abusing alcohol or a son who is constantly in trouble with the law, we may find it difficult to summon up daily the stamina to handle each crisis that comes along. When will it end? When can we finally relax and feel our children are safe?

It isn't easy to be patient in a society where instant gratification is the order of the day. Patience is anathema to our culture. Technology constantly finds ways for us to speed up. Fast food wasn't fast enough, so now we have drive-through windows. Who wants to stop and pay a toll on the highway? E-ZPass allows us to zip through in seconds. ATMs have eliminated the need to stand in line at a bank. Whatever problem we encounter, we want it solved now.

Unfortunately, modern technology hasn't yet figured out how to accelerate adolescence. The drama cannot be sped up by pushing a fast-forward button. We have to live each day as it comes.

In this chapter we will talk about the act of being patient, waiting for God's plan to unfold. Our three saintly models will be St. Monica, her son St. Augustine, and the bishop St. Ambrose, who had a great influence on both. These saints lived during the fourth century in northern Africa and Italy.

Once you have explored what Monica, Augustine, and Ambrose have to teach you about patience, we will suggest ways to put those lessons into practice. One way to put on the brakes is to make a pilgrimage, a religious journey that can open you up to change, revelation, and self-discovery. We will discuss the many ways to make a pilgrimage, ranging from a trip to a faraway land to visit a holy site, to an excursion to a church or shrine closer to home. There are even religious sites that you can visit online to receive guidance in prayer and meditation.

How long has it been since you prayed the rosary? Do you remember how the routine of repeating the prayers over and over again calmed and focused you? It's a sign of our hurried times that we see so few people in church fingering those sacred beads, head bowed, praying silently. You probably received your first rosary beads when you made your first communion and have them tucked away with your keepsakes in the back of a bureau drawer. Take them out today. If you have forgotten how to say the rosary, don't worry. We will refresh your memory so that you can refresh your spirit.

Another way to slow down our lives is by praying the stations of the cross. Most Catholic churches display plaques along their walls depicting Christ's journey to his death. Following along in his footsteps while praying will not only give us time to think, but also will help us regain perspective on our own problems. The last hours in Christ's life were the most hopeless that he had ever known, perhaps the most somber that humankind has ever recorded. Yet after that darkness, there

was light. If we can be patient, we will see the light at the end
of our suffering, too.

A COMPLICATED RELATIONSHIP

St. Monica, who lived from 332 to 387, is the church's
paragon of patience. For thirty years, she prayed for the
salvation of her son Augustine, who was struggling with inner
demons and resistant to the Catholic faith of his mother.
Because of her patience and persistence, she has become the
patron saint of mothers, particularly those who are attempting to parent an out-of-control adolescent boy.

It is easy to view Monica and Augustine in stereotypical
terms, him as the wayward son and her as the sensible,
devoted mother. (How many of us have cast those roles in
our own family?) Yet their relationship was a lot more complicated than that. The more we learn about these two
remarkable people, the greater insight we gain into our own
situation. Monica and Augustine were both very human.
Monica made many mistakes as she attempted to parent her
irrepressible son. There are some scholars, in fact, who believe
she may have exacerbated Augustine's problems by her constant attention. How many of us can relate to that behavior!

Augustine, on the other hand, particularly when judged
by modern standards, does not seem to have strayed so far off
the path. He had a wild time, to be sure, but how wild? In his
Confessions, the future saint condemns himself for "the
abominable things" he did, but he offers few actual details,
leaving us to wonder if he was as bad as he thought he was
or just a typical adolescent boy giving in to hormones and

urges. He was aware, however, of his mother's fears. "She was afraid for me even though I was not yet a Christian," Augustine says in Book II of *The Confessions*. "She saw the twisted paths I followed, those paths trodded by people who turn their backs to you, not their faces."

One thing about Augustine is clear: he was brilliant, a genius. His *Confessions* remains a seminal work that has influenced civilization, philosophy, and religion. His interpretation of the Scriptures was significant in creating many of the tenets we follow to this day, for better or worse.

So many of us are frightened by the alarming headlines regarding adolescents, particularly boys, who have become violent and even have killed. It becomes easy to overreact, believing our children are much worse than they actually are. Don't turn a blind eye to your child's failings, but don't be quick to panic, either. Read parenting books about adolescent behavior so that you understand what is normal and what requires attention. Talk to other parents to share information. In your zealousness to confront your child's problems, don't forget to praise the accomplishments, too. When you see progress, say so.

There was a basic goodness in Augustine that eventually came to the surface. Even though Monica was near despair worrying that her son was destined to go to hell, the common sense and solid values that she instilled in him won out in the end. This lesson is one that we all can hold on to. Our children need our prayers, yes. But we have to remember that despite what is happening with our children now, we spent many years teaching them right from wrong, encouraging them to strive for their best, and helping them learn from their mistakes. Those lessons may have been forgotten temporarily, but they are not lost.

In some fashion, our children may already realize that they have internalized our values and will ultimately return to them. The most famous quotation from Augustine's *Confessions*, his prayer to God, sums up this adolescent attitude: "Grant me chastity and self-control, but please not yet." How much of Augustine do you see in your own child? Sometimes adolescents will resist what we are trying to get them to do because they still feel the need to explore, express themselves, and, at times, misbehave. It's possible that Augustine would not have developed into the person (and saint) he became if he had not strayed. While no one can rejoice when a child gets into trouble, you can be encouraged by remembering Augustine's journey and the happy way it ended.

LIKE MOTHER, LIKE SON

One fact that is rarely mentioned about St. Monica is that she too once battled a demon: alcoholism. For this reason, her experience will resonate with parents whose substance-abuse problems may have preceded those of their children.

Many of the stories about Monica as a young woman mention an older woman who was her servant. This handmaid, who watched over Monica with the care and dedication of a parent, had a premonition that Monica's urges would soon get out of control. She is reported to have told Monica and her sister: "It is water that you are drinking now, because wine is not within your reach; but the day will come when you are married and find yourselves in charge of storerooms and cellars, and then water will not seem good enough; yet the habit of tippling will be too strong for you."

The wise servant's prediction came true sooner than expected. As was the custom in those days, Monica's family made their own wine. St. Augustine related in Book IX of *The Confessions* that St. Monica's parents routinely had their daughter collect wine from the cask by dipping a cup through an opening near the top. St. Monica got into the habit of taking a sip or two before she filled the decanter. In the beginning, according to St. Augustine, Monica sipped the wine not because she liked the taste but because of "a certain exuberance of youthful naughtiness, which is apt to erupt in playful behavior, and is usually curbed when it appears in children by the authority of their elders."

What happened next will sound familiar to many parents whose children began to drink at a young age. St. Monica began adding to those small sips, soon "quaffing near goblets-full of wine." Although the fact was unknown in Monica's time, we now know that adolescents can become addicted to alcohol quicker than adults. While it may take an adult ten or fifteen years to become an alcoholic, it can take anywhere from six months to three years for a teen to become addicted.

Perhaps Monica was a long way from becoming addicted, but, at the least, she was imbibing far too much alcohol for someone so young. Her parents apparently remained oblivious to her drinking. In his *Confessions*, Augustine says he ascertained that a higher power intervened to save his mother from her fate. Monica and a maid who often went along with her to fetch the wine began to quarrel. Speaking out in anger, the maid called Monica a "wine swiller," according to Augustine. "This shaft went home, and my mother took heed to her disgraceful conduct, condemned it and threw it off at once," he said.

Monica faced her growing physical dependency on alcohol as a young girl, before she was a parent. Yet many people reach adulthood still grappling with a substance-abuse problem. It takes courage, dedication, tremendous effort, and, yes, patience to combat an addiction, whether it involves cigarettes, alcohol, or drugs. It's easy for adults to make excuses for their behavior, saying no one else is being harmed by these bad habits. What happens, however, when children enter the picture? Even a young child is able to pick up signals. One mother who has battled a lifelong marijuana habit recalled that when her son was only six, he remarked to her: "Mommy, whenever you smoke that cigarette, you act funny." Her son eventually got involved with drugs himself, and, looking back, she regrets her own procrastination. She felt both shame and guilt for letting her habit get so out of control, setting a bad example for her son in the process.

Research has shown that there is a genetic link to addictive behavior. If alcoholism runs in your family, then your child stands a greater risk of becoming an alcoholic. If addictive behavior is a family trait, meet this challenge head-on. Ask for St. Monica's help in summoning the courage and patience you will need to face your possible physical dependency and your child's.

SHAKY MARRIAGE, WAYWARD SON

The whole time she was struggling with her impulsive son, Monica was also encumbered with a difficult husband. His name was Patricius, and he was chosen by Monica's parents to marry her. The best that can be said about Patricius is that he occupied a position of importance in his native city of Tagaste, in northern Africa. In terms of family responsibilities, however, he was hardly the parenting partner Monica needed to help her rein in their rambunctious son. First of all, he was a pagan and so wasn't about to assist Monica in her efforts to convert Augustine to Christianity. Second, he was much older than Monica, fifty-five years to her twenty-two when they married, a thirty-three-year difference. And third, he let Monica know early on that marriage would not prevent him from carrying on any number of sexual relationships that he had begun before his young bride arrived. In his pagan religion, promiscuity was not frowned upon but encouraged.

Aside from his affairs, the fact that Patricius did not share her faith created many hardships for Monica. Other young women in similar situations struggled as well. Their plight was captured by Tertullian, a Christian author who lived in northern Africa during Monica's times. According to Leon Cristiani, in his book *Saint Monica and Her Son Augustine,* Tertullian wrote: "How can a Christian woman serve God, if her husband does not worship Him? If she has to go to church, he will insist on meeting her at the baths earlier than usual. If it is time for her to fast, he will order a great feast for that very day."

Pagan husbands were often violent. Many a young wife, gathering water at the community fountain, hid her cuts and bruises behind a veil or scarf. Although Patricius has been described as an angry and violent man, Monica escaped his abuse by remaining silent in the face of his anger and praying for his conversion. In *Saint Monica and Her Son Augustine,* Cristiani says: "Her favorite weapon was patience. She said nothing. She waited until the fit of anger was over. She found a way of restoring her husband's composure after the storm."

Monica's way of handling her husband, dubbed her "conjugal strategy" by Augustine, seems submissive and humiliating when measured by modern standards. Yet for the times in which she lived, and the situation she was forced into,

Monica's plan was wise and ultimately worked for her. Her method even helped other women of her time who found themselves in the same situation.

Parenting a difficult adolescent often puts strain on a marriage or, if you are a single parent, on the relationship you have with your ex-spouse. Whatever your marital situation, you can draw strength and inspiration from Monica's example. We don't mean to suggest that women be submissive or men become domineering. Monica came up with a solution that worked for her. That's what you need to do. Whether you are a married parent, a single parent, a stepparent, or a relative grappling with the seemingly impossible situation of raising a headstrong child, there are people and resources out there to help you. Seek them out, as the other women sought out Monica's guidance. Pray to her that she lead you down the right path. Ask her for the patience and perseverance you will need to find a successful course of action.

How was Augustine affected by growing up in his home environment? In his *Confessions*, he is loath to criticize either parent for their unfortunate marriage. He reports his father's violent outbursts and drinking binges, so we can only assume that Augustine frequently witnessed Patricius's verbal lashings of his wife and Monica's stoic reaction. He came to admire his mother's patience and restraint. He mentions how other wives, seeing that Monica escaped abuse, sought out her advice. "Those who followed it found its worth and were happy; those who did not continued to be bullied and battered," he says.

However, Augustine did not escape unscathed. Throughout his life, he would remain conflicted about love, sex, and marriage. He took two mistresses, fathered a child, was betrothed but never married. Even while he continued to be sexually active, he longed for chastity. "The turbulence that drove him to such (alleged) extremes of lewdness and such extremes of (purely literary) self-abasement also drove him with equal force to discover the truth about himself," says Paul Strathern in his book *St. Augustine in 90 Minutes*. "Why did he behave in such a way? How could he be so utterly and despicably vile and polluted and at the same time yearn with equal longing for purity?" In his quest to find those answers, Augustine would stray far from the path that his mother hoped he would follow.

THE LONG WAY HOME

One mother posted this cry for help on our message boards at Parent Soup:

> *My daughter is thirteen years old. The last four months have been hell. Yesterday I came home early from work and found her smoking. She took some of my things and sold them to her new friends. I found a condom in her pocket. Every night we get into a fight. The other night she yelled at me that I love everyone but her. Not true, but she won't listen. What do I do now? How do I get her back?*

Another mother posted to offer reassurance: "Your story hit home. At thirteen, I was very much like your daughter. In fact, I had made the decision to be my mother's worst nightmare. I smoked, drank, went to parties with boys, and eventually, at age fifteen, ran away from home."

This woman said that through all her years of rebellion, her mother never abandoned her. "It eventually took my mother's tough love to wake me up," she said. After completing high school, she spent four years in the military. "I am now married and have a son of my own," she went on to say. "I hope and pray that my son doesn't take after me. My mom and I are closer than ever, and I apologize to her every day. I don't know what my mom had inside her to do what she did, but it worked."

Perhaps this mother had a little bit of St. Monica by her side to provide encouragement and inspiration. Monica's journey with Augustine was certainly arduous. The most difficult part was being patient with him as he resisted Christianity and explored other, somewhat dangerous, religions.

Because Augustine did so well in his studies, Patricius decided to send his sixteen-year-old son to Carthage, one of the great cities of the Roman Empire. Augustine was in a vulnerable state, looking for a way to reconcile his feelings with his beliefs. He happened upon the teachings of Mani, a third-century Persian who claimed to be the Holy Spirit and was killed by fire worshipers. Mani had founded a Christian-like religion called Manichaeism, which had been declared heretical by the Christian Church. When Monica discovered that Augustine had embraced Manichaeism, she was devastated. His action would be comparable to joining a cult today. How would she ever loosen the psychic bonds holding her son to this derelict sect?

Manichaeism held that the world was divided between good and evil. The Manichaean doctrine placed Satan on the same plane as Christ. In addition, the Manichaeans thought that each person possessed qualities of good and evil, was caught between God and Satan, and therefore would be powerless to manage any evil impulses. This religious viewpoint found an eager audience in Augustine. There he was, grappling with his human desires, which deep down he believed were evil. Along came a religion that provided an opportunity for him to escape blame. He could say, "The devil made me do it" and still be viewed as a God-fearing man.

At the time, Augustine was living with a mistress and had fathered a child. It is a measure of Monica's displeasure with Manichaeism that she was more willing to overlook Augustine's sexual exploits than his choice of religion. At one point, she was so distressed by his defense of the Manichaean beliefs that she barred him from her home in Tagaste rather than listen to his blasphemies. How many parents today have faced a similar crisis, banishing from their home a wayward child?

Yet Monica never abandoned her son. Even when he shut her out, she continued to pray, fast, and seek out the prayers of others to save her son. There's no doubt that Augustine, at times, felt hemmed in, although throughout *The Confessions* he never says one word against his mother. However, actions may speak louder than words. After Augustine announced his intention to journey from Africa to Rome to teach rhetoric, Monica followed him to the docks, hoping to dissuade him. In order to extricate himself from her grasp, Augustine convinced her that he would not leave until the following morning. She left to spend the night alone in prayer. Augustine, meanwhile, under cover of night, sailed away. The next morning Monica discovered her son's deception.

In Book V of *The Confessions*, Augustine came to terms with what he had done. "Like all mothers, though far more than most, she loved to have me with her, and she did not know how much joy You were to create for her through my absence," he wrote. Augustine was referring to his conversion, which, in retrospect, he now viewed as preordained by God. "She did not know, and so she wept and wailed, and these cries of pain revealed what there was left of Eve in her, as in anguish she sought the son whom in anguish she had brought to birth," he said.

In modern parlance, Augustine would have told Monica, "Mom, I need my space." When she refused to listen, he left anyway. Augustine needed time on his own, an opportunity to work through his problems and doubts without his mother peering over his shoulder. Perhaps you, like Monica, have felt betrayed by your child. But ask yourself honestly how many times you have backed your child into a corner so that there was no alternative for him but to resort to falsehoods and deceptions.

You are worried, and that is understandable. Sometimes, however, the timing needs to be right in order for God to work his magic. Monica discovered that, too.

At one point during her suffering, Monica sought out the counsel of a bishop—ironically, one who formerly had been a Manichaean. According to *One Hundred Saints*, this bishop told her, "The heart of the young man is at present too stubborn, but God's time will come. Go now, I beg you: it is not possible that the son of so many tears should perish."

The bishop told Monica the truth, although it was probably not what she wanted to hear. In retrospect, Augustine's journey to the dark side of religion was a crucial detour. During his time as a Manichaean, he did not cease to question every statement he encountered. He continued his quest for answers about the universe and himself. And when he found the Manichaean philosophy unable to satisfy his queries, he rejected those beliefs and moved on. Christianity now held a new appeal for him. Perhaps the explanations he sought had been before him all the time. Because he came to Christianity by such a circuitous route, Augustine became one of the religion's staunchest advocates.

We see many present-day Augustines around us, encouraging others to avoid their mistakes. We hear stories of criminals who have served their time returning to their neighborhoods to lecture young people to stay in school and get good jobs. Have you ever noticed how many people who now counsel others against substance abuse were once abusers themselves? These individuals are often the most forceful spokespersons for abstaining. They have traveled on the road to addiction and know that it leads to a dead end.

Monica would have been happier during her lifetime if Augustine had been compliant and immediately embraced his mother's religion. But then he probably would not have become one of the church's most outstanding scholars. We will never be able to understand what causes some children to stray and others to stay the path. We can never know God's plan. We can, however, draw solace from the example of these two saints. We can ask them for the patience we will need during any difficult twists and turns we encounter as we accompany our children through adolescence.

St. Ambrose—Mentor Extraordinaire

Both St. Monica and St. Augustine found comfort in the guidance of St. Ambrose, the patron saint of learning, who made it his mission to root out heresy and spread the doctrine of Christianity. St. Ambrose counseled St. Monica, encouraging her to remain strong and continue praying for her son, and mentored St. Augustine, talking with him during times when other adults, particularly his mother, were unable to reach him. Look around your own circle of relatives, friends, acquaintances, and professionals. Whom could you seek out for comfort and advice? Are there individuals—a religious leader, teacher, favorite aunt or uncle, trusted neighbor—who could intervene at the right time with your uncooperative adolescent?

St. Ambrose was certainly up to the task of serving as adviser and mentor. Ambrose's father had died when he was very young, so, like Augustine, he had been raised by his mother. That similarity in their backgrounds no doubt led Ambrose to be sympathetic to Augustine's struggles. At the same time, Ambrose had a great deal of love and respect for his mother, who raised not only him but also his sister, Marcellina, and brother, Satyrus, who also became saints. He could understand the daunting task facing a single mother, and Monica, in her efforts to rescue Augustine, was, for all practical purposes, operating as a single mother.

Early on, Ambrose earned the reputation of being a mediator. When Ambrose was about thirty-five, the bishop of Milan died, and the city was divided on naming a successor. In order to preserve the peace, St. Ambrose made a speech exhorting the crowds to make a choice. Impressed by Ambrose's presence and logic, the crowds began to chant, "Ambrose, bishop!" Ambrose tried to wriggle out of the responsibility, declaring that he had not yet been baptized. At that time Ambrose was serving as a governor for the provinces of Liguria and Emilia. The Roman emperor, Valentinian I, was so excited that one of his governors had been chosen as bishop that he encouraged Ambrose to take the position. Ambrose agreed. He was baptized and assumed his position as bishop for Milan.

Ambrose took to his new job with great enthusiasm and seriousness. He began to study the Scriptures and pored over the works of other religious writers. But he didn't lose himself in scholarly pursuits. He was always available to the people of his congregation, ready to help them with their problems and answer all their questions.

Ten years after he was named bishop, in the year 384, Ambrose became acquainted with Augustine. In Book V of *The Confessions,* Augustine reflected on his first impressions of Ambrose. He liked the bishop, commenting on his "fatherly kindness" and "charitable concern." But he was not immediately won over to Ambrose's way of thinking with regard to

Christianity. "I hung keenly on his words, but cared little for their content, and indeed despised it, as I stood there delighting in the sweetness of his discourse," Augustine said. Remember, at this time Augustine was somewhat obstinate in his belief that his mother's religion held no relevance for his life. Slowly but surely, Ambrose's oratories began to turn the tide. "As his words, which I enjoyed, penetrated my mind, the substance, which I overlooked, seeped in with them, for I could not separate the two," Augustine says. "As I opened my heart to appreciate how skillfully he spoke, the recognition that he was speaking the truth crept in at the same time, though only by slow degrees."

From this example we can understand that the relationship between a mentor and a mentee may take time and effort to develop. Don't be discouraged if someone you trust fails the first time to turn your child around. The important thing is for the mentor to establish a rapport with your child. Even though Augustine didn't immediately accept what Ambrose was saying, he kept listening. After a while, Ambrose's message sank in.

Soon Augustine began to find credibility in Ambrose's words. If Augustine had once found Catholic doctrine implausible and too simplistic for his intellectual prowess, he now saw, through Ambrose, that Catholic teaching had veracity and substance. "And yet this was the same religion as Monica's, the religion Augustine had learned from her as a young child," says Leon Cristiani in *Saint Monica and Her Son Augustine.* "It could not, therefore, be just an old wives' tale."

Monica soon followed her son to Milan. He told her that he was no longer a Manichaean but was not yet a Catholic. She was overjoyed to hear of his relationship with Ambrose. "She hurried all the more eagerly to church and hung upon Ambrose's preaching, in which she found a spring of water leaping up to eternal life," Augustine recounts in Book VI of *The*

Confessions. "She revered that man as an angel of God, for she realized that it was thanks to him that I had meanwhile been brought to my present point of wavering."

Monica had tried in vain for many years to get through to her son. Now here was someone else, a virtual stranger, delivering her message successfully. Monica could easily have become resentful. Yet her primary concern was the physical and spiritual well-being of her child. In her mind, God had answered her prayers by finding someone who could intervene on her behalf.

When you search for an Ambrose for your child, find someone who can convey your words in such a way that your child will open up and accept what he has resisted so vehemently in the past. Encourage your child to seek out Ambroses on his own, whether at school, on the athletic field, at church, or among other adults he meets. And when that person comes along, embrace his presence as a gift from God, just as Monica did.

A HOLY TRIAD—AMBROSE, MONICA, AND AUGUSTINE

Ambrose and Monica became the two most influential people in Augustine's life and, as such, had a mutual admiration. Augustine explained: "It was above all for the part [Ambrose] played in my salvation that she esteemed him; and he for his part held her in like esteem for her deeply religious way of life. Her spiritual fervor prompted her to assiduous good works and brought her constantly to church; and accordingly when Ambrose saw me he would often burst out in praise of her, telling me how lucky I was to have such a mother."

Ambrose's effect upon Monica was considerable. While in Africa, Monica had made it a custom to visit the graves of martyrs, leaving bread and wine as an offering. She attempted to do the same in Milan and was stopped by the cemetery door-keeper, who told her that Bishop Ambrose, hoping to discourage drunkenness, forbade leaving gifts of wine. Augustine, in Book VI of *The Confessions*, maintained that his mother only tasted the wine or, if she did drink, consumed only small sips. "What she sought to promote at these gatherings was piety, not intemper-ance," Augustine says. However, given Monica's previous encounter with alcohol, we have to wonder whether she came very close to repeating her earlier experience. In any event, Ambrose's edict removed that temptation. "It seems to me unlikely that my mother would have yielded easily over the abolition of this custom had it been forbidden by anyone other than Ambrose, whom she highly revered," Augustine says.

As the relationship of Monica and Ambrose illustrates, parents can likewise benefit from mentors. Keep an open mind with regard to the mentors in your child's life. Perhaps you could also learn from listening to and watching this role model. Your relationship with your child's mentor can be rewarding, but remember that he or she is primarily in your life to help your child. Refrain from using the mentor as a spy who can report on your child's comings and goings. If the mentor loses credi-bility with your child, the relationship will falter and perhaps fail.

LETTING GO

Perhaps the biggest challenge in parenting is knowing when to let go. That task becomes doubly difficult when your child has gotten off to a shaky start. If your parenting responsibilities have seemed to resemble a search-and-rescue operation, you may worry that your child will never be able to function with-out you in an emergency.

Yet Monica's experience shows us that the time will come when we can let go. For her, that moment came in August 386 when Augustine announced that he was ready to embrace the Catholic faith. His conversion did not lack for drama. Ponticianus, one of Augustine's friends, had come to visit from North Africa. They were in the garden of the villa where Augustine and Monica were staying, and Ponticianus was talking about his fellow soldiers and their time in Treves, where they were accompanying the emperor on his chariot races. Ponticianus said he and the other soldiers began reflecting on their goals. "Have we no higher hopes than to become the emperor's friends?" they wondered. "And what good will that do? Why not become friends of God?"

"These words loosed a veritable tornado in Augustine's heart," says Leon Cristiani. "This is what he had been asking himself over and over: What is life all about? Why are we on this earth? And in what mire I have lived so far!"

After Ponticianus departed, Augustine, in his grief, returned to the garden to seek relief from his agony. "I flung myself down under a fig-tree and gave free rein to the tears that burst from my eyes like rivers, as an acceptable sacrifice to you," Augustine says in Book VIII of *The Confessions*. "Many things I had to say to you, and the gist of them, though not the precise words, was: 'O Lord, how long? How long? Will you be angry forever? Do not remember our age-old sins.'"

Then something remarkable happened. Augustine heard a small childlike voice exhorting him: "Pick it up and read; pick it up and read." He racked his brain trying to think of what child's rhyme he might be hearing but could come up with nothing. He then recalled how St. Anthony had been instructed by a Gospel text to go and sell his possessions and give the money to the poor. Was it possible the Lord was reaching out to him in this manner?

He went to the area where he had been sitting with his friends and retrieved the book of St. Paul's letters that he had been reading. The book was open, and he read the first passage he found: "Not in dissipation and drunkenness, nor in debauchery and lewdness, nor in arguing and jealousy; but put on the Lord Jesus Christ, and make no provision for the flesh or the gratification of your desires."

In that instant, Augustine was converted. "I had no wish to read further, nor was there any need," he said. "No sooner had I reached the end of the verse than the light of certainty flooded my heart and all dark shades of doubt fled away."

There are so many lessons we can draw from this description of Augustine's conversion. First, never underestimate the positive power of peers. Augustine's friend Ponticianus, through the telling of his tale, provided a spark that fired up Augustine's spirit. When a child is having problems, we are naturally suspicious of her friends. Are they leading her astray? Don't lose sight, however, of the positive impact friends can have. Peer influence is a powerful weapon.

Second, there is force in the written word. Seeing in the Scriptures Paul's condemnation of worldly desires helped Augustine take a stand. Use the written word to sway your own child. A book such as *Go Ask Alice,* about a teenager's descent into drug abuse, may have more impact on your child than your entreaties to abstain.

From the time of his epiphany until his baptism on Easter 387, Augustine lived at the villa and prepared for his entry into the church. We can only speculate as to Monica's joy during this time, finally seeing that her son would be okay. No doubt she was weary from all she had endured. As she told Augustine: "For my part, my son, I find pleasure no longer in anything this life holds. . . . One thing only there was for which I desired to linger awhile in this life: to see you a Catholic Christian before

I died. And this my God has granted to me more lavishly than I could have hoped, letting me see you even spurning earthly happiness to be his servant."

Monica knew when to let go. Cynics might say that because so much of her life centered on her son and his salvation, her life was devoid of purpose once Augustine became a Christian. Monica would argue that she was performing God's work in converting her son. And once God's work was finished, so, too, was her time on earth. Monica died in 387 in Ostia, on her way back to Africa with Augustine.

However you interpret Monica's choices, ask for her guidance so that you will be able to slowly loosen the bonds that tie you and your life to your child's. Seek her assistance so that you will not neglect the other people and things around you while you struggle with your child. This request is particularly important if you have other children whose needs may not be as pressing as those of your troubled child but are no less significant.

Slow Down One Step at a Time

It's easy enough to want to be patient, but slowing down isn't something we can merely will ourselves to do. Have you ever waited for water to boil? Or stood in line at the bank when you knew you had dozens of other errands awaiting you? Being forced to wait can be excruciating, even when what we are waiting for is inconsequential in the grand scheme of things. When we are waiting for a child to see the light, being patient seems like an unattainable goal. How do we slow down? What can we do?

For one thing, we can take a pilgrimage, putting our thoughts and energies into a physical and spiritual activity that is demanding and definitive. "With a deepening sense of focus, keen preparation, attention to the path below our feet, and respect for the destination at hand, it is possible to transform even the most ordinary trip into a sacred journey, a pilgrimage," says Phil Cousineau in his book *The Art of Pilgrimage: The Seeker's Guide to Making Travel Sacred.*

The word *pilgrimage* comes from the Latin word *pelegrinus*, meaning foreigner. The first definition for *pilgrim* given in the dictionary is "a person who travels about; wanderer." The second definition adds a religious component: "a person who travels to a shrine or holy place as a religious act." Our reference point is apt to be the pilgrims who came to America for religious freedom and are now the centerpiece of our Thanksgiving Day celebration.

According to Cousineau, the earliest recorded pilgrimage was made by Abraham four thousand years ago, when he left Ur to venture into the desert in search of God. Since that time there has been a virtual stampede of religious adherents making journeys near and far to seek out truth and peace while visiting birthplaces of holy men and women, sites where miracles reportedly occurred, and churches and cathedrals housing relics of various saints.

Pilgrimages became particularly popular during the Middle Ages, so much so that Cousineau characterizes these journeys as the beginning of tourism as we know it. That analogy is a good one because we can easily see how we might view a pilgrimage as a vacation away from the tension and turmoil in our lives. "Integral to the art of travel is the longing to break away from the stultifying habits of our lives at home, and to break away for however long it takes to once again truly see the world around us," says Cousineau. A short pilgrimage can even be incorporated into a longer vacation, a moment of calm in what might be a hectic sightseeing schedule.

A pilgrimage can be a solo quest or a group activity, and it doesn't have to deplete your bank account. It can be as simple as taking a walk in the woods, drinking in the quiet, marveling at your environment, and reading from a religious book recently lent to you by a friend. The important thing is that the journey takes you away from your current suffering and to a peaceful place where you can restore your energy and spirit.

There may come a time, however, when you will be ready to take a faraway journey to a religious location you have longed to see, such as Mexico City, where the first apparition of the Blessed Virgin Mary to be sanctioned by the church occurred in 1531; Lourdes, France, where St. Bernadette saw the Virgin in 1858; or St. Peter's Church in Vatican City.

Beverly Donofrio, in her book *Looking for Mary*, recounts her relationship with the Blessed Mother and her experience of traveling to Medjugorje, Bosnia, where the Virgin has been appearing for the past twenty-three years. A fallen-away Catholic, Donofrio happened upon a painting of the Virgin Mary at a yard sale, and soon her home was filled with images of the Blessed Mother. Donofrio, who had given birth to her son when she was seventeen, had always felt she failed as a mother. After suffering what seemed to be a permanent rift with her son, she sought solace in the Virgin. Perhaps the mother of Christ could teach her how to be a good mother to her son, she thought. Journeying to a land where our Lady had been spotted seemed like the most logical step.

Donofrio experienced more than one miracle during her stay in Bosnia. On a Saturday, she went with other pilgrims to sit on a hill where each month the Virgin appeared to Mirjana, a local woman. "I close my eyes and try to feel Our Lady's presence, and what I feel is hard to describe," she says. "It's like the feeling you get when you've spent the entire day outdoors, in nature. . . . [A] feeling like you're floating."

Later, when she returned to the house where she was staying, some women on a balcony called out to her to look at the sun. She found it spinning like a pinwheel, radiating sunset colors in all directions. "I know that I'm lucky and blessed," she says. "I'm being given signs to help me believe, to strengthen my faith."

Your pilgrimage may not be as dramatic as Donofrio's, but it may prove to be exactly what you need right now. "Pilgrimage is the kind of journeying that marks just this move from mindless to mindful, soulless to soulful travel," says Cousineau. "It means being alert to the times when all that's needed is a trip to a remote place to simply lose yourself, and to the times when what's needed is a journey to a sacred place, in all its glorious and fearsome masks, to find yourself."

THE ROSARY: A DIRECT LINE TO MARY

Whenever the Virgin Mother appears on earth, her message is clear and succinct: Pray the rosary. For parents who are caught up in the despair of worry over a child, repeating the prayers of the rosary will not only earn you points with our Lady, but also will have a calming effect. Rote recitation is a form of meditation that helps us soothe our mind and body and confront daily tasks with a more positive attitude.

The physical rosary looks like a necklace, with fifty-four beads spaced at regular intervals in a circle and a short tail of five beads with a crucifix hanging off one end. Young people have been known to wear rosaries as ornamentation, but the true purpose of the rosary is for prayer. You can say the prayers of the rosary—the Hail Mary, Our Father, Glory Be to the Father, Apostles' Creed, and Hail, Holy Queen—without having a physical rosary to follow. Mary, Queen of the Universe Shrine, in Orlando, Florida, has become well-known for promoting the finger rosary, a metal ring outfitted with ten balls and a medal that allows the wearer to say the rosary unobtrusively, while commuting to work, for example.

Saying the rosary involves going around the beads four times, saying twenty decades (or sets of ten Hail Marys) while meditating on the mysteries. The mysteries of the rosary are events from the life of Jesus and Mary that are to be meditated upon as we make our way through the prayers. There are four sets of mysteries (including the recently added luminous mysteries), each comprising five events. The joyful mysteries include the annunciation of the Blessed Virgin, the visitation of the Blessed Virgin to St. Elizabeth, the nativity of Jesus in the stable at Bethlehem, the presentation of Jesus in the temple, and the finding of the child Jesus in the temple. The luminous mysteries include Jesus' baptism in the Jordan, the Cana wedding, the proclamation of the kingdom, the Transfiguration, and the first Eucharist. The sorrowful mysteries include the agony of Jesus in the Garden of Gethsemane, the scourging of Jesus at the pillar, the crowning of Jesus with thorns, Jesus carrying the cross to Calvary, and the crucifixion of Jesus. The glorious mysteries include the resurrection of Jesus, the ascension of Jesus, the descent of the Holy Spirit upon the apostles, the assumption of the Blessed Virgin into heaven, and the coronation of the Blessed Virgin in heaven.

To say the rosary, start at the "tail" of five beads and the crucifix. Bless yourself with the crucifix and say the Apostles'

Creed. On the first large bead, say an Our Father; on the next three beads, say three Hail Marys; and on the fifth bead, say a Glory Be to the Father. Begin the first decade by saying an Our Father on the large bead and then announcing the first mystery. Say ten Hail Marys while reflecting on that mystery, and end the decade with a Glory Be to the Father in the space between the last bead and the next large bead. Continue this pattern through all twenty mysteries. Each time you complete five decades (one set of mysteries), say the Hail, Holy Queen. (For the complete text of the prayers, see the appendix in the back of the book.)

FOLLOWING THE PATH OF CHRIST

The rosary with its mysteries echoes the stations of the cross, another exercise we can use to slow ourselves down while getting closer to Jesus. If we are caught up in our own suffering, making the stations of the cross allows us to refocus by reflecting on Jesus' sufferings, what he gave up for us.

Following Jesus' death and resurrection, many pilgrims traveled to Jerusalem to visit the sites associated with him. After a time, these holy sites became fixed stops on a pilgrimage, but soon it became difficult for people to visit them in person. Beginning in the 1500s, duplicates of the way of the cross were created in towns across Europe. Over time, the stops along the way became standardized as the fourteen stations of the cross we know today:

Jesus is condemned to death.

Jesus carries his cross.

Jesus falls the first time.

Jesus meets his afflicted mother.

Simon of Cyrene helps Jesus carry his cross.

Veronica wipes the face of Jesus.

Jesus falls the second time.

Jesus meets the women of Jerusalem.

Jesus falls a third time.

Jesus is stripped of his clothes.

Jesus is nailed to the cross.

Jesus dies on the cross.

The body of Jesus is taken down from the cross.

Jesus is laid in the tomb.

A closing reflection on the resurrection of Jesus may be added.

There are many ways to make the stations of the cross. If your church has plaques for each station on its walls, you may stop at each one, reflect on the image, and pray. You may make the stations with a group or alone. If you are led by a priest through the stations, special prayers will probably be included. Usually booklets are passed out so that you can follow along. The priest recites certain prayers, and participants respond at the appropriate time. The priest may also add his own comments at each station and then encourage everyone to pray silently before moving on.

If you haven't made the stations of the cross recently, you will be surprised at the impact this exercise can have on you, particularly now, when you are going through your own period of suffering. At each stop you can take time to contemplate Jesus' agony while offering up your own suffering.

For many of us, as for Monica, the rewards of our labors may be a long way down the road. We have to believe that, at some time in the future, our children, like Augustine, will be okay. All it will take to get us through is the patience of a saint like Monica.

Prayer to St. Monica

Dear St. Monica, you, more than any saint, understand the suffering that can come from being a parent. Your life was made richer through your son St. Augustine, but not before you were forced to endure many trials. Help me, dear saint, be patient with myself and my child. Strengthen my spirit so that I may find the courage to face whatever hardships come my way. Fill my soul with love overflowing, and remind me that, in the end, a parent's love can conquer all. Ask your dear son St. Augustine to watch over my child, to keep serious dangers away. Implore St. Ambrose to send my way other adults who possess his wisdom, tenderness, and capacity for reaching the youthful heart. Amen.

Saints Who Inspire Patience

St. Monica can help you remain patient with your difficult adolescent.

St. Augustine can encourage you that even wayward children find their way home.

St. Ambrose can remind you that you need not shoulder this burden alone.

Discussion Questions

1. Often we are impatient with our children because our lives move so fast. Can you think of ways to purposefully slow down your pace (for example, standing in the longest line at the store, praying silently while you wait)?

2. We are quick to criticize our children and slow to praise them. Have you missed opportunities to comment on something positive your child has done?

3. St. Augustine said, "Grant me chastity and self-control, but please not yet." Think back to your own adolescence. Can you relate to what Augustine said?

4. Monica's parents allowed her access to wine at a young age, and this availability led to her experimentation. Have you provided your child with similar opportunities (for example, allowing a glass of wine or champagne on special occasions, leaving liquor in places where it can be easily obtained)?

5. Do you have an addiction you haven't faced? How could doing so now benefit your child?

6. Monica and her husband, Patricius, had different views on religion, marriage, and parenting. Inevitably, these differences sent mixed signals to Augustine and complicated Monica's efforts to parent him. How could you and your spouse or parenting partner resolve some of your differences in order to parent more effectively?

7. One of Monica's strategies for avoiding confrontations with her husband was to hold her tongue until his anger had subsided. What methods can you employ within your family to encourage everyone to cool down during disagreements?

8. Augustine tricked his mother, leaving Rome without telling her. He needed time alone to think. How often do you give your child space to be alone? How can you restrain yourself from constantly intervening in your child's life?

9. Like Augustine, adolescents often question their faith, even sampling another religion or belief. How can you manage your own child's detour without becoming overbearing?

10. Ambrose tackled his job as bishop of Milan with dedication yet always had time for his people, including Monica and Augustine. If you have a full plate, how do you make yourself available, physically and emotionally, to those who need your help, advice, and love?

chapter six

Serenity

*Keep your soul peaceful. Don't ever trouble
yourself with the bad things that aren't your
fault; you will do infinitely more good
if you were to be calmer.*

—BLESSED ANNE MARIE JAVOUHEY

P arenthood and worry go hand in hand. We forget that.
From the very moment God delivers a baby into our
arms, we feel unbridled joy, an overwhelming sensation
of love, and its underbelly: worry. The spanking-new mother
just out of the delivery room and the adoptive mother cradling
the child for whom she has waited for so long—both understand the word *miracle*. Still, for every ounce of promise there
is a weight: the threat of harm, illness, misfortune. From a
baby's first sighs to the parents' last breath, the love that mothers and fathers have for their child is always balanced by an
equal measure of worry.

How your child fares in the bassinet, in school, and in life
colors every day, every month, every year. As if knowing
instinctively about this link between your child's well-being
and yours wasn't enough, now researchers offer sobering
proof. Carol Ryff, a psychologist at the University of
Wisconsin-Madison, conducted a study that revealed this cor-
relation: how happy adults feel later in life depends on how

well their offspring turn out. In other words, a parent's ultimate satisfaction with life hinges on his or her children's successes or failures.

What kinds of successes? Ryff says, "We found that how emotionally well-adjusted the children were—how their marriages turned out, for example—tended to have a stronger influence on parents' positive self-regard than did the jobs they attained." And mothers tended to be more influenced by how their sons turned out than by the fate of their daughters.

If you are grappling with a troubled young adolescent, you already know that your sanity is tethered to your child's state of mind or state of affairs. Fixing things is no longer as simple as bandaging a bleeding knee or distracting a disappointed child with a lollipop. When toddlers turn into teens, the bruises get more complicated. Trouble festers. Adolescents choose situations that cause them and their parents anxiety. For instance, an unplanned pregnancy befalls your daughter or your son's girlfriend. Or your child develops an eating disorder. As the parent, you feel your child's terror and turmoil. Life becomes monopolized by anxiety, dread, apprehension, and even horror. Ironically, sometimes your best efforts to bandage, cure, or heal your troubled child rub salt into his wounds.

In the middle of a serious family crisis, how does a parent, like the following one, cope?

> *This has been the worst time in my life! My sixteen-year-old daughter always told me, "I am a good girl." We talked often about morals, boys, dating, peer pressure, the importance of getting a good education, and just about life. My daughter was at a house where the police answered a domestic-disturbance call. She was in the company of her newfound friends. All had police records,*

and all were under seventeen years of age. One boy is under house arrest, with an ankle bracelet to prove it. Apparently my child was attacked by a fifteen-year-old. In all the commotion I still don't understand exactly what caused the incident. The police brought my daughter home. I thought this was the end of the crisis.

A few nights later, several of these boys came into my house and took my daughter, along with all her belongings, to the truck parked outside. I wasn't home. Then these friends called to tell me that my child will not be returning home. My daughter says she just wants to have fun and have no rules and no "leash" around her neck.

I am a single mom. Dad has not been in her life for many years. I know she's angry. I'm told this is rebellion. But I am panicked about what could happen to her. I pray to God to keep her safe. I am sick to my stomach all the time. I can't eat. I cry every day. I don't know what to do.

Having a child run away is a nightmare. The majority of young adolescent runaways are actually younger than this particular girl. Thirteen is the most typical age. "These are youngsters searching for someone to help them understand themselves," explains James Garvin, a renowned expert on early adolescents and author of *Learning How to Kiss a Frog.* "People who cannot handle stress often run. The running is a symptom of a person who does not see himself [or herself] as worthwhile or loved or forgiven or adequate."

The tragedy of runaways like the girl in the story is that they leave behind people who care. Even mothers and fathers who have failed at conveying that message love their children. When a child runs away, the parent remains home alone, with only the ghost of the troubled child. Home alone in the grip of endless sleepless nights. Host to an overactive imagination sketching one disaster after another. The imminent danger facing the adolescent bolter didn't cross her mind. Yet the danger tortures the parent left behind.

To that mother, to you, to any parent in a crisis, the concept of serenity may seem out of place at first. To choose peace of mind over worry seems wrong somehow, like abandoning a child in an hour of need. Does a parent deserve serenity at a time like this?

The answer to that question is absolutely! Even though it seems as if God has stood by and allowed catastrophe to enter your family, he doesn't want you to live in a state of eternal anxiety. No one understands your excruciating state the way God does. He carries the weight of the world on his shoulders. As the Father of all of us, he sees human suffering every day somewhere around his globe: hurricanes, floods, starvation, sickness, war.

When you feel panicked by your emotional burdens, imagine how heavy God's load is. When you are locked in dread about what may befall your child, reflect on God's dread on the night before his Son's crucifixion. He has been inside your own nightmares. He knows what your darkest hours look like and feel like. He has had his own. And your darkest hours are his, too.

Because God understands so intimately the panic parents experience, he envisioned a road to serenity for you. God whispered words of wisdom into chosen ears to outline the path clearly. He gave one of his angels a powerful set of wings to carry you above the fray. He permitted certain of his children to experience agonies and others to experience miracles so that the lessons of serenity shine through.

In this chapter, you will meet the saints with the secrets to serenity and be invited to the places where peace on earth is possible, if only for a day.

St. Benedict: The Saint
Who Ran Away

St. Benedict ran away, and his story serves as a guide. It validates the importance and healthfulness of serenity as a spiritual quality and delivers a plan anyone can follow.

The exact year of St. Benedict's birth is hazy, but it is believed to be around 480. Benedict came from a good Roman family who lived in Nursia. When he reached early adolescence, his parents sent him off to Rome for a well-rounded education. As a student in post–Roman Empire Italy, Benedict met up with lots of wild and rowdy contemporaries. The countryside and towns, ravaged by warfare, crawled with ruthless folks who picked homes clean and terrorized innocent people. Christian leaders seemed more like pagans and atheists because their lives smacked of greed, lust, and gluttony. The church itself seemed overrun by heretics and arguments.

When Benedict looked around, he became fearful. Could he resist peer pressure from fellow students to indulge in drinking, wild sexual encounters, stealing? Would he get sucked into these amoral ways? Rather than remain in the ruinous city and risk becoming spiritually contaminated, Benedict opted to flee Rome. He literally headed for the hills.

Benedict walked to the outskirts of his town and climbed further up into the hills until he reached a wild and rocky terrain known as Subiaco. Benedict chose a cave in a desolate cavern. There, a monk named Romanus befriended him, gave him sheepskin clothing, and brought him bread. Benedict lived like this for three years.

Eventually, word spread about Benedict's holy and spartan lifestyle. Students and disciples joined him in this hermit life, away from everything and everyone but God. Benedict organized those followers and built twelve monasteries. Together they formed a religious order known as the Benedictines.

Had Benedict found spiritual peace? Not yet. A jealous priest targeted Benedict. First he spread lies about him. Then he sent him poisoned bread. When neither of those tactics destroyed Benedict's work, the priest sent sexy and enticing women to seduce the monks. To save his monks from further temptation, Benedict decided to leave.

He and his monks set off for Monte Cassino, a once-thriving town that now lay in ruins, sacked by the Goths. All that remained were temples where pagans offered sacrifices to the gods Apollo and Jupiter. Benedict fasted and preached and eventually converted the townspeople. He built another monastery there, and the sacred groves once devoted to pagan idols were reconsecrated as oratories to St. John the Baptist and St. Martin of Tours.

At Monte Cassino, Benedict set down his prescription for monastic life. Called the Rule of St. Benedict, his plan for his community of reclusive monks focused on liturgical prayer, study, and work. Benedict never became an ordained priest but remained a layman. While the world around his monasteries descended into what became known historically as the Dark Ages, Benedict constructed a parallel universe of order and structure. His outposts became oases of civilization, Europe's last remaining centers of learning, art, and law.

Benedict lived in chaotic times, and his monastery continued to be plagued by troubles even after he died. During his lifetime, he foresaw Monte Cassino being destroyed by the barbarian Lombards. After his death, it indeed was razed. It was restored, only to be sacked again by another horde, the Saracens. After being rebuilt a third time, Monte Cassino stood undamaged for many years. Then, during World War II, it was thought to be a Nazi headquarters and was bombed and razed again.

In the war's aftermath, people rummaged through the rubble. They discovered remains that turned out to be Benedict's body and that of his twin sister, Scholastica. Two peaceful souls found amid the ruins.

A RULE BOOK FOR SERENITY

Benedict's life was a quest for serenity. He ran from turmoil toward God. The monasteries he established became enclaves of sanity and hospitality, as well as emotional and spiritual sanctuaries, during the Middle Ages. Within their sheltering walls, Benedict designed rules that became the framework for building a life of serenity. The instructions for his fellow monks resembled what we would call today a how-to book. He outlined schedules and spiritual principles for them to live by.

The Rule of St. Benedict defined monastic life with the elements of silence, solitude, detachment, meditation, labor, chastity, community, and obedience. While they were developed for monks, his monastic routines and principles can be adapted for use by any distressed parent. Benedict offers you a sanctuary, a refuge, an oasis in the midst of your inner terror.

Let's explore some of these principles of monastic life that anyone can follow. We will talk about them in the context of our modern world and explore how these principles can deliver you from your personal problems.

Silence

The Rule of St. Benedict cultivates silence. In the monastery, a period of silence began at 8:00 p.m. and continued until 8:00 a.m. the following morning, when Mass was celebrated.

Our culture advertises the opposite of silence. Parents, spouses, business managers—we all are advised to talk everything out. Therapists urge us to dredge up and confess every grudge or gripe we feel. *Communication* is the buzzword. This supposedly magic exchange is thought to guarantee a happy family, a solid marriage, a productive workplace, a true friendship.

A parent who lives with a troubled child (or even a healthy normal teenager) knows all too well that communication can be the expressway to arguments. Silences become the silent treatment, anything but soothing.

It's time to look at silence the way Benedict did—as a choice. Set words aside temporarily. Let yourself experience the stilling of the mind and body that comes with not talking. Experience silence as relief from the war of words that tears so many families apart.

Solitude

In our world, solitude is rare. The global village touches everyone's life, no matter how remote. Computers, the Internet, TV, and radio connect us and entertain us twenty-four hours a day.

Idleness—long considered the "devil's workshop"—was once something to be avoided. Today it seems that no one even has time to be idle. Instead our mantra is "There aren't enough hours in the day." Think about it: when was the last time you uttered that hectic refrain? Whether it happened an hour ago or a few days ago, chances are that you, too, are overwhelmed by a schedule of appointments, activities, and responsibilities.

Time alone is also characterized as negative. Called loneliness, it is misconstrued as the absence of love or failure at relationships. Sometimes we turn it into a punishment. We exile a defiant child with "Go to your room and stay there until you know how to behave."

The truth is that solitude is as vital a human need as connecting is. Nature programmed us to spend time alone by making sleep—our body's downtime—a necessity. In our waking hours we need time alone, too. It is within these precious personal bounds that we can connect with our soul and with God. Solitude rejuvenates us; it blocks out the busy world and the problems that bombard us. Seek out some private time in a private place. Let solitude restore your equilibrium and ground you in this hectic world.

Detachment

A by-product of solitude is letting go, detaching yourself from everyone and everything else. Detachment is easier said than done. Silence isn't so hard; you can close your mouth and even bite your tongue if you feel the urge to talk. And solitude can be relatively easy to achieve. You can march off into the great alone, be it the country or the privacy of a bedroom, or you can schedule time away from the members of your family or your friends. What is most challenging of all, especially for a worried parent, is letting go of your inner turmoil.

Detachment needs to be physical, emotional, and intellectual for it to qualify as a spiritual state. Without mastering detachment, you will never achieve peace.

Even once you realize that you need a break from worrying, embarking on that journey to detach yourself is not easy. You are fraught with second thoughts. You are reluctant to let go. If you drop the ball of vigilance, if you lose sight of your responsibility, will more disaster befall your child? You may find yourself immobilized by this line of reasoning.

So you take a step backward, focusing again on the fate of your child. You go over the latest events and rehash the details. You check and recheck. It's that same reflex that makes you double-check the lock on the front door one more time, or go back into the house to make sure you turned off the oven or the lights in the bedroom.

When you find yourself in these circumstances, not feeling right about abandoning those thoughts about your troubled child, turn to St. Raphael the archangel. He is the patron saint of travelers and can be trusted to watch over your child while you venture toward restoring your spiritual equilibrium.

St. Raphael: Angelic Child Care

St. Raphael has the double distinction of being an angel—even one of the seven archangels—and a saint. Archangels are pegged a spiritual cut above the other angels, elevated because of their special responsibilities. As one of the seven archangels, Raphael sits at God's throne in the company of two other famous archangels, Gabriel and Michael.

Raphael means "remedy of God." St. Raphael is famous for fixing situations and solving problems. The following story from the Bible's book of Tobit illustrates St. Raphael's celestial skill.

As the biblical tale goes, Tobit felt apprehensive because his son, Tobias, planned to cross the desert alone. Tobit wanted to go along but hesitated. After all, he was blind, and how much protection could a blind father offer? His companionship might be more of a hindrance than a help. So Tobit called upon Raphael to accompany his son on his journey.

For the adventure, Raphael disguised himself in a human form. The archangel even gave himself a human name, Azarias. Azarias guided Tobias safely across the desert. Then he steered Tobias toward Sarah, a widow seven times over.

Sarah had been praying to St. Raphael, who also has the reputation of being an angelic matchmaker. Those searching for a life partner seek him out. Sarah had a romantic history that certainly called for divine intervention. She had married seven men, one after another, and each one had died on their wedding night at the hands of a demon. Sarah wanted to marry again. Not surprisingly, none of the eligible men in town proposed.

St. Raphael, as Azarias, introduced Tobias to Sarah. Tobias became smitten with her. Being a newcomer, he didn't have an inkling about Sarah's marital woes. When the two fell in love and decided to marry, her father, Raguel, had a heart-to-heart with Tobias, explaining what had befallen the other grooms. But Raphael had instructed Tobias on how to avoid the fate of the last seven suitors. Tobias needed to pray for three days, go fishing, burn the innards of the caught fish, and think of God on the wedding night. The wedding, under Raphael's tutelage, went off without a hitch.

Tobit learned that his son had arrived safely and had entered into a happy marriage. St. Raphael had answered Tobit's and Sarah's prayers, killing two birds with one stone.

St. Raphael the archangel is the perfect saint to seek out when worry over your child is holding you back from advancing on the path to serenity. Ask St. Raphael to watch over your child the way he watched over Tobias. With this archangel on guard, you can concentrate on your own spiritual plight with a clear head and a lighter heart. Your wayward adolescent will be in good hands. And St. Raphael might even surprise you by doing more than you ask.

Meditation

With the boundaries of silence and solitude set and detachment engaged, you are ready for meditation. Turn your thoughts to something that will enhance your spiritual growth. Review the life of a particular saint. You've read many stories in the preceding chapters.

One of the best meditative exercises is clearing your mind entirely. Emptying your mind makes room for God. By meditating you invite God and his grace into your silent and welcoming heart. Once you clear your mental storehouse of worry, God restores you with the spiritual resource of his love. Spending time in God's company and striving for communion with him will bring you to a place of peacefulness. He will renew your strength.

Finally, take the prayer for serenity at the end of the chapter and read each line slowly until the sentiments carry you away.

Labor

Throwing yourself into a physical task serves a valuable function. It occupies you, mind and body. It engages you and becomes an escape, leading you toward serenity.

What type of task accomplishes this? It must not be an activity that you associate with anxiety. For instance, if you tend to feverishly vacuum a room or furiously rearrange every item of clothing in your bureau after a fight with your child, those tasks aren't appropriate. They merely focus the tension on something else. You want to break the cycle of tension.

Choose a neutral task to lead you toward serenity. It could be as simple as sorting through your old recipes, parting with instructions for the orange-cranberry torte from 1989 that you know you will never master. Or it could be setting aside an afternoon or evening and actually attempting that orange-cranberry torte, remembering which old friend or grandmother handed it down to you.

Yard work is always an option. No matter where you live, or how small your yard is, or what season it is, there are always outside chores. Planting a vegetable patch in the spring, raking leaves in the crisp autumn air, or shoveling snow or pruning a tree in the late winter—whatever the chore, it often leads to a relaxing rendezvous with nature.

If you decide to tackle the land, consult with St. Fiacre, the patron saint of gardeners. Fiacre was born in Ireland into a powerful Celtic family. Rather than follow in the footsteps of his father, who was a chieftain, he entered a monastery. Eventually, Fiacre traveled to France, where the bishop of Meaux granted him land for his very own hermitage.

Fiacre built himself a hut in which to live and cleared some of the countryside. He felt compelled to take care of the sick and feed the hungry, so he harvested food and grew herbs and flowers for medicinal purposes. Gardening became the cornerstone of his ministry.

According to legend, Fiacre realized he needed additional land because more people needed food and care than he originally thought. He went to his bishop. The bishop issued a bizarre edict: he told Fiacre he could have as much acreage as he could turn over with his shovel in one day.

If you have ever turned over your garden with a shovel, you know how backbreaking it can be, and slow. Fiacre knew his human limitations, so he prayed for guidance. The next morning his gardening ability turned miraculous. Like Moses magically parting the Red Sea with a wave of his hands, Fiacre toppled trees and uprooted bushes merely by dragging his shovel behind him. Stones popped out of the dirt, and trenches appeared. The bishop awarded Fiacre the huge parcel of land he had miraculously plowed.

What about city folk? you may be thinking. Not to worry. Nearly all urban areas now have community gardens where green-thumbed residents gather to sow vegetables and flowers and reap a harvest of rewards. There are numerous community projects to clean up parks or restore areas that have gone to seed. And although you may live in the city, perhaps a friend or relative doesn't. Mowing, sowing, and clearing don't have to be done on your own lot. Once you look around, you will see tasks that need to be performed everywhere.

Sleep

Benedict's regimen didn't order a good night's sleep. We include it because getting adequate rest is essential to achieving calm. Many parents with a troubled adolescent rarely get a good night's sleep. The following mother, who lives with a teen she describes as "out of control and repeatedly truant," explains:

I cry every day. I try not to. In the daylight hours, I hold back tears that feel as if they could choke me. I know that I have to be strong. I have to go to work. I am a teacher, and I have to face other people's children. Still I am sick to my stomach nearly all the

*time. When I get into bed at night, it takes me forever
to fall asleep. I can't stay asleep because even my sleep
gives way to sobbing.*

Being sleep deprived is expected when you are the parent of
an infant. New mothers and fathers share fatigue war stories.
Bleary-eyed, in between yawns and stretches, they reminisce
nostalgically about how it felt to get a full night's sleep. For
these newly initiated caretakers, sleeplessness is an admission
into parenthood, a badge of honor, a blessing. Being awakened
by an infant's cry is hard, but once you lay eyes on that tiny
miracle, the loss of sleep seems inconsequential.

Losing sleep over an adolescent has no such charm. A parent who tosses and turns over a teenager has no supporting cast
with which to compare fatigue tales. If you do confess at work
that you are exhausted because you spent last night worrying
about your son's failing grades, or waiting at a police station,
your listener is not likely to nod and utter, "Me, too. I know
how that feels." So you don't explain. You live with the fatigue
that weighs you down more heavily each night.

You can't change a problem with an all-night fretting vigil.
Furthermore, being overtired makes you less effective. When
you are sleep deprived, you are more inclined to lose your temper, feel hopeless, and make bad decisions. Stress creates sleeplessness, which compounds your distress.

If you suffer from sleeplessness, examine bedtime routines
in your home:

- Do you get into arguments with your teenager late in
  the evening? Many parents do. They can be over
  homework or bedtime. Few of us realize that young
  adolescents stay up later because they are physiologically programmed to do so. They stay up late not to

goad us or sabotage themselves the next morning, but because they really are too alert to fall asleep.

- Do you allow bedtime to become worry time? "I actually call 11:00 p.m. my 'worry hour,'" one woman admitted to us. "Like clockwork, as soon as I turn the TV off and put the lights out, I don't have visions of sugarplums dancing in my head or sheep jumping over fences. Problems appear. How can I get through to my daughter tomorrow? Should I do this or that? Next thing I know, it's midnight, and I am farther away from falling to dreamland than I was an hour ago."

Recognize your mistakes. Revamp your habits. Replace them with these guidelines: Go to bed at the same time every night. Rise at the same time every morning. Calculate how many hours of sleep you need to feel well rested. If you can't always get a good night's rest, catch up by sleeping later one day a week.

If you continue to struggle with sleeplessness, pray to St. John Ogilvie. His martyrdom underlines the torture of insomnia. John, the son of a Scottish noble, became a Jesuit in France during the 1600s. While a vocation to join that order didn't always entail danger, it did during this particular era. At that time, the Catholic Church was banned in Scotland. When John secretly returned to Scotland to do missionary work, he courageously went about his calling. But his cover was blown. He was arrested and tried for no less than treason. The Jesuit "traitor" endured the torture of being kept awake for days.

St. John Ogilvie knows that being denied a good night's sleep is cruel and inhuman punishment. You can summon him to rest alongside you and lull you to sleep.

The Retreat Experience

Annual retreats have always been commonplace experiences for parochial high school students. A class travels to a cloistered setting. The purpose is to disconnect from the classroom and connect with spirituality. Speakers raise spiritual issues and, hopefully, consciousness. Quiet contemplation is encouraged, though sometimes young people do more giggling and whispering than praying.

Retreats for adults, once popular as well, have fallen on hard times. Formerly busy retreat locations have seen their business wane. Oddly enough, health spas, offering a more secular oasis, have replaced religious retreats. The spa experience focuses on basic issues of well-being, nutrition, and exercise. Spas advertise low-fat gourmet meals, facials and body wraps to soothe and relax, and physical workouts to jump-start metabolism. The soul is addressed, but the body takes center stage. Such an approach falls short of the real essence of a retreat, which is to move beyond one's surface and go deeper within.

As you seek serenity, resurrect the retreat experience. A retreat need not be limited to only what your parish offers. The important thing to remember is that a retreat is any experience that allows you to set aside personal time and space to escape your life and try out Benedict's rules.

Retreats can be structured in any number of ways, depending on an individual's desires. Surely one will fit into your life. All you have to do is look for the one that offers you the right combination of solitude and detachment and holds out the potential for contemplation. Here are several suggestions.

A Parish Retreat

Many parishes schedule the occasional "Day of Recollection," a daylong spiritual event built around prayer and meditation. Your parish may also advertise workshops, a modern term for and take on a retreat. If your church does not hold retreats, look into a neighboring community parish. You can even explore what kinds of seminars other denominations might have.

Your parish's office will be able to steer you to possibilities in your region. Regional religious magazines are another good source. These advertise retreats scheduled by monasteries or convents in your area. If you attend a retreat elsewhere, share your experience with your local parish. It might encourage them to bring back retreats.

A Traveling Retreat

Some people have to literally get away in order to find peace. Many find it appealing to travel to a place that embodies the elements that St. Benedict championed.

One such retreat explorer is Paul Wilkes, an author who admits a lifelong fascination with monastic life. He decided to leave behind his routine each month and spend time at a Trappist monastery called Mepkin Abbey. Once a rice plantation located on the banks of the Cooper River in South Carolina, Mepkin Abbey became his escape. In search of spiritual secrets within this abbey's walls, Wilkes believed his monthly visit could have lasting value. If he frequently visited simplicity, prayer, silence, and community, perhaps he could mine those intangible secrets and bring what he discovered to life outside the cloistered walls. His experience turned into a treasury of insights, which he included in a book called *Beyond the Walls: Monastic Wisdom for Everyday Life.*

You've seen already how many people hit the road with spirituality as much on their agenda as sightseeing. A careful read of travel sections in magazines and newspapers will reveal that a growing number of tourists design vacation time to incorporate spiritual aspects. Religion and recreation are intersecting.

Europe teems with possibilities for retreats. Convents, like Rome's Casa di Santa Brigida, are being rediscovered. Established in the fourteenth century as an inn and hospice on the Piazza Farnese, Casa di Santa Brigida is home to nuns in the Order of the Most Holy Savior (or Bridgettines) and is also the place where the Swedish-born St. Bridget died.

Bridget, the cousin of a Swedish king, married early and bore eight children (one of her daughters would become St. Catherine of Sweden). After her husband died she took religious vows and founded her order in Sweden, but she didn't stop there. Bridget traveled to Rome in 1350 to agitate against the evils of the Roman Catholic Church at that time.

Casa di Santa Brigida has a spiritual geography. It houses a special sense of quiet and perhaps even a ghostly residue of grace. The sparsely furnished rooms, antique furniture, and lithographs of St. Peter preserve life the way it looked during Bridget's time. Even St. Bridget's room has been meticulously kept up, right down to the thick wooden tabletop upon which she died.

Dining amidst the current cloistered nuns, taking time on a begonia-laden roof garden—all can be part of the experience of a retreat at Casa di Santa Brigida. A locale like this offers inspiring surroundings and history and the potential for a vacation spot to turn into a spiritual refuge.

A Home-Based Retreat

To make a retreat, you don't need an international itinerary, a car, or even a church. You can make a retreat in the privacy of your own home. Set aside time, either a Saturday or a day off during the week. If you cannot spare an entire day, don't let that be an excuse. You can isolate an afternoon, a morning, or an evening. Turn the answering machine on. Warn friends and family beforehand that you will be unavailable.

With St. Benedict as your guide, write a schedule for your special private time. Gather a few selected readings. Schedule an activity that falls within that definition of manual labor. Most important, give yourself over to silence and solitude.

As Paul Wilkes reminds us in *Beyond the Walls,* "Finding a perfect geographical space is often not possible. But inner space ever awaits our bidding. The interior cloister sets our soul on solid ground so that we need not (indeed, cannot) frantically thrash about, diffusing our energies, failing to see the graces that abound for the soul wholly present. Such graces are often obscure. But in the interior cloister, that place of solitude and silence, we may enter into this holiest of holy places when God awaits us."

Your retreat is a time to pray and to do, but it is also a time to sit still. Parents gripped in family melodramas find themselves stalked by anxiety. Prayer has a tendency to become one long plea for help. This time, don't ask for anything. Don't even talk to God. Just listen. When there are no words, the silence can be filled with God's presence. If you let yourself just be a receiver of messages, not a sender, you will become a receptacle of his powerful love and solace.

A Cyber Retreat

Cyberspace is the newest frontier for inspiration, with Web sites designed to provide you with resources for an online retreat experience. If you are private and progressive, an electronic retreat might be the avenue for you. All you need is your personal computer and a commitment to follow the suggested instructions. With a pledge of time, attention, and dedication to the exercises, you can find virtual serenity.

One example of an online retreat is Creighton University's "34-Week Retreat for Everyday Life," established by the Collaborative Ministry Office. On their Web site, they explain how it is possible to make an online retreat:

> *A retreat is a RETREAT FROM our ordinary patterns and a RETREAT TO a "place" where we can be more receptive to the graces God wants to offer us. This online retreat affords us the opportunity to check this site each week and receive some guidance for our retreat from and to. Some of us have access to the Web both at work and at home. We can print the weekly pages and review them each week. And because it will be "one week at a time," all we need to do is take advantage of the weekly Guide, with its options and exercises (http://www.creighton.edu/ CollaborativeMinistry/r-how.html).*

Sitting at the keyboard, you can type and click your way into a virtual world of silence, solitude, and detachment. You can sign on to a community of like-minded souls or opt for a solitary experience. Sites like this offer a wide array of reflections, Scripture readings, and advice—all at your fingertips.

A Walking Retreat

In the midnight hours, you find your mind going round in circles as you try to figure out the best course of action to take on behalf of a child. You are driving in the car, and you miss your turn because you are so distracted. You open a book and find yourself reading the same paragraph over and over again. You feel you are always going in circles, with no way out.

Coincidentally, physically going around in circles is being prescribed as a way to center oneself. Labyrinths, which provide the circular framework for this activity, are being touted as one of the newest (and oldest) tools to acquire a spiritual focus, a sense of peace, and intimacy with God.

In *Walking a Sacred Path: Rediscovering the Labyrinth as a Spiritual Tool,* Episcopal priest and psychotherapist Lauren Artress offers labyrinth experiences like this person's: "I was aware, as I walked along, how I slowed down, how everything else faded away except the path, and of the adventure of the thing."

A labyrinth is an intricate, winding pathway of concentric lines that usually has about seven 180-degree turns, or circuits. A labyrinth walker is supposed to follow the pathway of concentric lines to the middle, where traditionally he or she should pause, quiet the mind, and allow thoughts to flow naturally. As the walker then moves out from the center, the goal is to process the insights gained during this exercise.

Labyrinths have played an important spiritual role in many cultures worldwide for centuries. Going back more than thirty-five hundred years, this Christian image and a family of derivatives have appeared in places such as Peru, Iceland, Scandinavia, Crete, Egypt, India, Sumatra, and the southwestern United States. In medieval Europe, the labyrinth represented for Christians the one true path to eternal salvation. In Sweden, fishermen would walk a labyrinth before setting off on the sea to ensure good catches and favorable winds. Unwelcome winds supposedly would be trapped in the coils of the labyrinth. It became a popular religious symbol. The familiar symbolism of the labyrinth has surfaced throughout history in many mediums: wood carvings, woven designs in blankets and baskets, landscaped village greens, stone patterns in the desert and on shorelines, mosaics and tile patterns on flooring in cathedrals, churches, and villas.

Now labyrinths are making a comeback. The latest labyrinth walks are being constructed in hospitals and health-care facilities. In the current mind-body philosophy of healing, labyrinths offer patients a walkway to better health through spiritual healing. For those unable to walk, portable map-sized labyrinths have been created to be explored with the fingertips or traveled with the eyes only.

Labyrinths also come on canvases that you can unfold and lay out on your floor. Or you can construct your own labyrinth by tracing a pattern in the sand by the shoreline or in a field of dirt. In *Exploring the Labyrinth: A Guide for Healing and Spiritual Growth,* Melissa Gayle West gives instructions for how to build one from rocks, rope, and other materials.

Experiment with a walk around a labyrinth. As the popularity of this ancient practice increases, look for labyrinths in your community medical centers. For more information, contact the Labyrinth Society, in New Canaan, Connecticut, and ask for a copy of the *Journal of Labyrinths and Mazes.*

(A labyrinth is not a maze. A maze is a puzzle, offering many choices along the way. A labyrinth is not a puzzle, but a single pathway to peace.)

Your retreat—whether you escape within a circular path, the electronic highway, a distant locale, your local community, or a self-imposed cocoon—can succeed. As you willingly peel away all your psychic layers of helplessness and hopelessness, your worry and terror, you are uncovering your spiritual center. The harder you work toward exposing your soul to God, the easier life becomes. Once you travel to that oasis of your spiritual core, you will realize just how lifesaving and empowering it can be. God is there to grant you the respite you need. Peacefulness, even amid battle zones, will restore your spirit and rearm you with strength to overcome your crosses.

St. Ignatius of Antioch: A Saint for Desperate Times

The last saintly lesson comes from St. Ignatius, who found serenity in the most impossible circumstances. Ignatius was one of the earliest bishops of Antioch in Syria, the second or third as far as history can tell. He's thought to have been a disciple of St. Peter, St. Paul, or St. John. One of the original martyrs, Ignatius puts a face on the persecution of Christians in the Colosseum, where Christians were sent to be devoured by wild beasts in public games. The Roman emperor Trajan condemned Ignatius to this fate in 107. Ignatius found himself carted off to Rome.

The road trip took him though Smyrna and Lystra before crossing into Europe. Apparently Ignatius had lots of days and nights to think. He traveled inward even as his body journeyed toward a horrific end. He tapped into his faith. He began writing letters—seven, to be exact—which have survived.

Did those letters implore his enemies to spare him? No. Ignatius bypassed the drama in this world that crackled around him. Instead he occupied himself with the other world—the spiritual drama. He underscored that his fellow Christians should pledge unity, seek community, and celebrate the Eucharist.

When Rome lay just over the horizon, did Ignatius write in code so that Christians would ambush his captors and set him free? No—quite the contrary. He addressed his last letter to the Christians in Rome. In it, Ignatius speaks gently and patiently, telling his supporters in Rome not to try to get him a reprieve. He says, "Let me follow the example of the suffering of my God."

Ignatius managed to drape himself in silence and solitude, to detach himself and meditate, even in the face of his grisly martyrdom. His accomplishment in the fatal climax of his days can inspire us. In your most anxious moment, pray to St. Ignatius to show you his way.

Finally, know this: God does not want you to suffer. Even though he allows you to be bombarded with misfortunes, he makes available many different pathways toward peace. Even while he sees into your being and recognizes the anxiety overwhelming you, he holds out the ways and the means for you to quell that panic. He has instructed saints like Benedict, Ignatius, and Fiacre to model for you how to find a way through life's terrors, tragedies, and trials. Serenity is a gift within your reach. All you have to do is reach out to God, and it will be yours. A refuge is available. Put all your anxieties out of your mind so you can focus on communicating with God. The saints will keep you company, especially the ones you invite to help you.

SERENITY'S SPILLOVER

In the face of a crisis, if you temper your anger, defuse your anxiety, and master your panic with the tools of silence, solitude, and detachment, you are helping yourself. Yet there is also an additional effect. You are modeling valuable coping mechanisms for your child. You are setting an example that demonstrates the value of spiritual tactics. Such lessons are not lost on adolescents. Consider the story related by this mother:

> *I, too, have an adolescent daughter caught shoplifting. She, too, has acted hateful and horrid toward me. She, too, can be very mouthy. It starts like this: she wants something or wants to go somewhere, and I say no. She goes into a tirade. She continues, and I send her to her room. My advice to you is, first of all, try to get away from her for a little while. Time-outs aren't just for our children. We all need to disengage at times. Second, turn a deaf ear to her nasty remarks. Ignore what she says. She is only trying to push your buttons. Just tune it out. Do not, I repeat, do not get into a shouting match. You will never win. Silence is the much better retort. At a later time, admit the way she treats you hurts. Good luck, and a lot of prayer always works.*

When you are able to find a refuge even in the midst of an argument or a crisis, you are blazing that trail for your child. Serenity is possible, and only one person in your life needs it more desperately than you do. That person is your child.

Prayer for Serenity

Dear God, you whispered the words of serene wisdom in the breeze blowing through St. Benedict's cavern. You infused the archangel Raphael's wings with the power to carry us above our terrors. You permitted St. John Ogilvie to suffer just so he would be receptive to our night terrors. You empowered many others with miraculous abilities so that we know miracles exist even when the world seems most unmanageable. Just as you have whispered to the saints before us, whisper to me so that I may find a moment of peace. If I take that first step into isolation, into the garden, into the church, let the next step closer to you be easier to make. If I still my voice and erase my worries, fill me up with the sound and illuminating warmth of your love. Put your arms around me, and surround me with your peacefulness. If I offer up my broken heart to you, heal it in this moment with the calming gift of your love. Communion with you is all I need at this moment and forever. Amen.

Saints Who Can Guide You toward Serenity

St. Benedict can be called on to help you at every turn as you work toward serenity.

St. Raphael will stand in for you so you can take a break from your stress.

St. Fiacre can become your companion in the outdoors.

St. John Ogilvie can keep you company during sleepless nights.

St. Bridget can inspire you to see that it is never too late to begin focusing on your spirit.

St. Ignatius of Antioch can be your guide when you feel most desperate.

Discussion Questions

1. Are you living in a constant state of anxiety because your child is gripped in melodrama or misbehavior? Can you conquer your child's demons or cure her illness for her? No, the challenge is hers, not yours. Think carefully: could your anxiety be making things worse for her?

2. All seven of Sarah's husbands died before she asked the archangel Raphael for guidance. If you have tried grounding your child and taking away privileges without success, to whom can you turn for a different perspective on your dilemma? A parenting group? A counselor at your church?

3. Has worry sentenced you to sleepless nights? How does your child sleep? Sleep deprivation can make anyone more short-tempered and volatile. Read a how-to article on getting a good night's sleep, and share the tips with your teen.

4. A family in crisis is a recipe for emotional chaos. While you can't resolve your problems easily, would creating physical order and harmony in your household have a positive impact? Hold a family meeting to create a few new routines and rules. Install shelving for clutter; designate a quiet hour; assign a child a fun job, such as creating a dessert every Friday night; post a bulletin board. Schedule a powwow in a month to ask, Are things better?

5. When your child secludes himself in his bedroom, are you suspicious? Do you assume he's up to no good, or wasting time goofing off? St. Benedict ruled silence and solitude to be a critical part of spiritual life. Rather than nag, shouldn't you be cultivating personal time and space for everyone, including yourself?

6. Both St. Benedict and St. Fiacre found solace in gardening. The physical labor monopolized their energy, and nature's beauty inspired their awe. Could you create a garden, a vegetable patch, or a window box or participate in a community green project? Could you involve your child as well?

7. Parents know that riding in the car with a child can open the way for intimate conversations. Can you recall the last time you and your family took a road trip that involved hours of driving time? If not, plan one. The traveling might take you into more private territory with your family members.

8. Do you write in a diary, keep a journal, or frequently confide in a good friend? Do the entries and confidences consist of your venting about trials and tribulations with your child? Could this be multiplying instead of relieving your distress? Try imitating St. Ignatius of Antioch. On the way to his martyrdom, Ignatius wrote letters of advice and encouragement to others, not self-defensive missives. Does changing the subject help you lighten your load?

9. Does your panic ever turn to anger that you spew toward heaven? Do you ever curse God or feel like cursing him? Have you ever considered that God is your ally in anxiety? Can you list the ways that God has suffered tragedy? Start with the death of his only Son.

10. Do you expect an end to worrying about your child? Is this expectation realistic? Do parents ever stop fretting?

chapter seven

Truth

While truth is always bitter,
pleasantness waits upon evildoing.

—ST. JEROME

It's a sin to tell a lie. But many parents lie to themselves and to others when they are unable to face the terrible truth that they have a child who is troubled. It takes courage to tell the truth. How much easier it is to avoid confrontation, look the other way, and deny what is happening. Yet eventually we will pay the price for our duplicity.

Why do we lie? We hope to preserve the harmony in our household. Accusing a young person of wrongdoing is never an easy task. As parents we want to believe the best about our children. It may be tempting to overlook warning signs. Sure, she has a new coat in her closet, and you know her allowance is long gone. But shoplifting? Your daughter? You may suspect, but you don't know for sure. Why rock the boat? And once you look the other way, it becomes easier to do so the second, third, and fourth time around.

If you are currently struggling, you may try to hide your household turmoil from your extended family. You may fear that if your relatives knew the truth, they might criticize how you have raised your child. You may be particularly sensitive if you have siblings or cousins whose children are model citizens.

How many more times can you hear that Suzy is headed for Harvard and that Evan is about to be drafted by the NBA? What good news do you have to tell? And what does that say about the job you have done raising your child?

Don't be too hard on yourself. No one starts out to be a bad parent. In this day and age, parenting is more difficult than it once was. The youth culture creates an environment that defies the values we try so hard to instill in our children. It isn't possible to isolate your child from all the evil forces in our world. It takes more than just shutting off the TV set. You may be parenting under circumstances that are beyond your control. How could you have known that your home life, and your child's, would be rocked by divorce, joblessness, illness, or death? Any of these events may have been enough to throw your child off track. Cutting yourself off from family, telling everyone half-truths, or dodging questions with evasive answers may deprive you and your child of needed support at this critical juncture.

Perhaps you are afraid to confide in a friend or someone outside of your immediate experience. In the back of your mind, you hear a recording from your own childhood: "What happens in the family stays in the family." What could be worse than having your acquaintances and coworkers gossip about your hardships to one another? You blanch when a companion asks: "So how is Debbie doing in school?" How can you reveal that Debbie was expelled from her second school, and you are afraid she will never complete her education? Rather than be truthful, you give a noncommittal answer and quickly move the conversation in another direction.

Sometimes we avoid the truth because we are protecting our own image in the community. This strategy is often adhered to by professionals, such as doctors, lawyers, psychologists, or educators, who fear their credibility will be tainted when the truth comes out. These people don't want their neighbors, patients, or business associates to know that they have an out-of-control child. Yet covering up soon exacts a huge toll. It takes a great deal of mental and physical energy to hide the truth. When people finally discover your secrets, you may find that they have had similar experiences and are more than willing to help out. Even without a common bond, your friends may offer up help, comfort, and support throughout your trials.

One lie inevitably leads to another. St. Peter learned this lesson well when he lied three times that he didn't know Christ. Later, he went and hid because he was so ashamed that he had abandoned our Lord. Similarly, when you avoid confronting your child about alcohol or drug use, skipping school, or stealing, you are deserting a loved one at a time of dire need. Confronting the truth is never pleasant, but it is the right thing to do if you truly care about your children.

In this chapter we will confront lies, both large and small, and explore ways to strengthen resolve and stop evading the truth. Many of the saints knew the value and the price of telling the truth. During the early years of Christianity, numerous saints were put to death for refusing to hide their religious orientation. It would have been so much easier to lie to avoid execution, yet many saints, including St. Agnes, St. Dorothy, and St. Julia, refused to denounce Christ and were martyred. Blessed Kateri Tekakwitha was forced to flee her Native American village because she had embraced Catholicism and refused to lie about her action. And Blessed Sebastian Valfre remains an inspiration to all of us in our efforts to become more truthful. With these holy men and women as our guides, we can pray that we will find our own way to the truth and that we will be positive role models for our children, encouraging them to do likewise.

We will prod you to rediscover the sacrament of reconciliation, known to us throughout our childhood as confession.
Many Catholics are still uncomfortable with the updated version of confession, where one can sit rather than kneel and talk
with a priest rather than merely recite a litany of sins. We will
pull open the curtain on the modern-day confessional and tell
parents how they can use this all-important sacrament to begin
a truthful conversation with God. In many parishes, the congregation celebrates reconciliation together. We will give guidance on how a family can use this ceremony to reconcile their
own differences and come together with renewed hope.

During adolescence, many young people seek out privacy
and may avoid confiding in parents. A teenage girl facing an
unplanned pregnancy may live in terror that her parents will
find out. A teenage boy who has become addicted to tobacco
may need his parents' help to stop but may be fearful to solicit
their aid. Fear of punishment is a major reason why a teen
hides wrongdoing. Focusing on the climate of forgiveness cast
by reconciliation, we need to convince our children that they
can always come to us with the truth. As God offers us unconditional love, so we need to offer the same to our children.

CONFRONTING THE TRUTH ABOUT
OUR CHILDREN

Facing the truth about your wayward child is bound to
make you miserable in the short term. You can expect disrup-
tion in your home and perhaps intrusive questions from
friends. However, getting the facts out into the open is the necessary first step in setting your child straight. You can continue

to turn your back, but your child's problems won't go away. In fact, chances are that with every day that goes by, your child's situation will only get worse until a major crisis occurs, forcing you to take action.

That's what happened to this mother:

My fifteen-year-old daughter ran away three weeks ago. I should have seen it coming. Lately, she has been screaming a lot. I also know that she was depressed over a boy. She was involved in a dispute with him that turned physical. He hit her, and the police were called. Even after that, she decided to run away with him. They came in the middle of the night and moved her stuff out. I just know that she will end up pregnant. I was a single mom, and her father has never been in her life. I know she is upset about that. We should have talked more, and I should have gotten her help so she could deal with her issues. Now I fear it may be too late.

Another woman, a stepmother, posted on our message boards about her troubled stepdaughter. At the time, she still had a chance to help her stepdaughter. But she hesitated. Did she also wait too long?

My fifteen-year-old stepdaughter is using marijuana and drinking and smoking. I found out by reading her journal. Now what do I do? Her mother is ill, and [my step-daughter] has recently come to live with us. I don't want to rock the boat, and I'm fearful that if I confront her, our relationship will be ruined. I can't count on my husband (her father) to take the lead. He has convinced himself that his daughter is an angel and won't hear the truth about what she has been up to. Any advice?

If you are afraid to face the truth about your child (or if you, like the stepmother above, have the unenviable task of helping a parenting partner face the truth), call upon the child-saint Agnes for courage. Only thirteen years old when she was martyred in the year 304, Agnes is often regarded as the model of bodily purity. While no one disputes the fact that she was killed because of her faith, many feel the details surrounding her death have been embellished throughout the ages. Nonetheless, she remains one of the most popular saints of the church, and her name is one of several mentioned in the canon of the Mass.

What we do know is this: Agnes was very beautiful and had many young men eager to claim her hand in marriage. She turned them all down, vowing to remain a virgin for Jesus. One suitor, Eutropius, son of the Roman governor, was angry that he had been rejected and reported to his father that Agnes was a Christian. Eutropius no doubt hoped that the governor would be able to do what he had failed to accomplish, namely, convince Agnes of the folly of her ways and encourage her to take him for her husband. Eutropius's father tried, but even in the face of his authority, which one can imagine would have intimidated many a young adolescent, Agnes remained firm in her decision to save herself for Christ. The governor took a tougher line, threatening Agnes with imprisonment, torture, and, ultimately, death, but she could not be moved. Legend has it that various instruments of pain were paraded before her— iron hooks, stretching racks, boiling oil, razor-sharp swords— to no avail. She made light of these threats, totally astonishing the most hard-hearted of her accusers.

St. Ambrose observed: "Girls of her age usually can't even bear a parent's angry glance. They cry at needles' pricks as though they were wounds. Agnes, however, faced her persecutors fearlessly."

Exasperated, the governor had Agnes stripped of her clothing to be paraded in shame through the streets of Rome. Her hair miraculously grew long and full, covering her nudity. When she arrived at her prison, a house of prostitution, Agnes was greeted by an angel who clothed her in a radiant white garment. She was placed before men who were told to satisfy their most wicked desires. Again, Agnes stood up to her tormentors, declaring that Christ would never allow her to be violated in such a manner. Instead, anyone who gazed upon Agnes was so overcome with her beauty and purity that she remained untouched. Eutropius was the one young man who did attempt to be rude to her. He was struck blind on the spot. Upon the pleas of his companions, Agnes restored his sight.

Thwarted at every turn, the governor finally ordered that Agnes be executed. She said, "You may stain your sword with my blood, but you will never be able to profane my body, consecrated to Christ." A nervous soldier carried out the judge's order and with one swift blow beheaded Agnes. Her body is buried a short distance from Rome.

Because Agnes sounds like the Latin word for lamb, *agnus,* this saint is often pictured with the animal. On her feast day, January 21, the pope blesses two lambs that are then cared for until their wool is sheared. The wool is then woven into sacred garments sent to archbishops throughout the church.

Let Agnes's courage inspire you to acknowledge and take control of your own situation. Pressured as a young teen, she understands the temptations that have caused your own child to go off track. Ask her to intervene with your teenager, just as she intervened when Eutropius lost his sight. Right now your own child is "sightless," and St. Agnes can help restore his vision of what is right and wrong. But the process must start with you. Don't back down. Have the courage to confront the truth and the strength to deal with the consequences.

TELLING THE TRUTH
TO OUR CHILDREN

Did you have a turbulent adolescence? Did you experiment with drugs? Did you sneak behind your best friend's garage to have a smoke after school? In college, were you more often to be found drinking at the local bar than studying in the library? Were you arrested as a youth? It may have been for something so silly that you cannot remember why or how you got into trouble. Were you sexually active as a teen? Did you take risks you know were foolhardy, and do you still marvel that you didn't wind up a teenage mother or father?

If you were totally honest with yourself right now, you would admit that your child's behavior scares you because it reminds you of your own transgressions. You know you are lucky to have survived, but you worry that your child may not be so fortunate. You also may be feeling guilty. Perhaps God is punishing you for your mistakes by giving you a child who is repeating your behavior. Can the old saying "The apple doesn't fall far from the tree" be true? Watching your child, are you witnessing a reincarnation of your youthful self?

Just like hair color and nose size, certain behaviors are inherited. There is a genetic link to alcoholism, for example. Children of alcoholics are three times more likely to become alcoholics than children whose parents show no sign of this addiction. If both parents are alcoholics, the risk is even greater.

We all come into middle age with baggage from our childhood and young adulthood. Some of this psychic paraphernalia comes from our relatives, but some of it we have collected on our own. How can we get our children to clean up their acts if we have not upgraded our own? Are there things concerning you that you still are not truthful about—your drinking, for example? If you are still hiding your "stash," hoping your son won't find your marijuana, don't bother. He already knows you smoke, and that may be why your admonitions to him fall on deaf ears. Like father, like son. Like mother, like daughter. That comparison can be good, or not so good.

Are you providing your child with a worthy role model? St. Dorothy's parents did. In fact, her parents were hard acts to follow. Both of them died as martyrs. Dorothy didn't have to follow their lead, but she did. When the authorities came for her, she bravely professed her belief in Jesus Christ. Not surprisingly, she was pressured to recant. Two evil women were assigned the task of converting her. Instead, she converted both of them to Christianity. The judge presiding over her case was furious and ordered various tortures to weaken her resolve. She was jailed, burned, and subjected to stretching. Nothing could force her to lie about her devotion to Christ.

Finally, the judge ordered her beheading. On the way to her execution on a cold winter's day in the year 303, a bystander named Theophilus taunted her. "Bring me some apples or roses from heaven, won't you?" he jeered at Dorothy. After Dorothy's death, a small child holding apples and roses appeared to Theophilus. "These are from Dorothy," the child said. Theophilus then believed, converted to Christianity, and himself died a martyr.

Chances are that Dorothy would have died a martyr even if her parents had not shown her the way. Their example, however, inspired her. They could have hidden their religion from her, thinking they would have been protecting their only daughter from certain death. They didn't. They trusted her with their secret.

Have you been hiding your own secrets from your child? You may think that by doing so you are sheltering him from harm. The opposite may be true. Now is the time to share some of these family confidences. Revealing truths that have remained hidden for so long will be a difficult, and in some cases painful, exercise, but you may help your child avoid serious mistakes.

You don't need to practice full disclosure. Everyone is entitled to privacy. You may want to skip some of the more sordid details. But if you had (or have) a drinking problem, then you must warn your child that she is susceptible, too. If you had a brush with the law, a devastating encounter with a designer drug, or a pregnancy scare, share your experience with your child. You may prevent her from making a future mistake.

If your child came to your family through adoption, he will not be affected by your family genetics. But what legacy has been left to him by his birth parents? Do you know the details? Perhaps some of his acting out can be attributed to his anger and frustration over not knowing the truth about his background. Don't think that because he isn't asking about his adoption he isn't thinking about it. (For more information on adolescents and adoption, refer to *Who Am I? . . . And Other Questions of Adopted Kids.*) It's time to share with him the information you have, no matter how difficult it may be for him to hear. Keep this in mind: what he is imagining is far worse. He needs to know the truth.

Most of all, when you tell the truth to your child, confront the truth yourself. If you have an addiction problem, deal with it. Unfinished business from your past makes it impossible for you to parent objectively. Seek professional help. Do it for your child. Do it for yourself. Pray to St. Dorothy that, like her parents, you can become the kind of parent you want your child to emulate.

Confronting the Truth, Then Letting Go

Some people have no problem telling the truth. If anything, they are zealous in their honesty. They tend not to discriminate, either, among the people who become their (often reluctant) audience. Family members and close friends are included, of course. But these truth tellers are just as comfortable blurting out the shameful tales of their lives to complete strangers. Sit on a bus next to one of these confession-driven individuals, and you are likely to hear her life story.

Like a rubber tire caught in a rut, these people can't seem to get over the hump. They are truthful, yes; but their inability to leave the past behind sabotages any plan they might have for the future. They constantly bemoan their fate and look for people to blame. Over time, their attitude may prove to be debilitating for their children. How many times can a young adolescent hear "When I was your age I never . . ." or "My parents would have whupped me if I had . . ." or "If my father hadn't died . . ." or "You don't know what hard work is . . ."? Each of those statements may be true, but the words smack of resentment, envy, and anger. Chances are the child will shut down before the mother or father has finished even one sentence. And after he has heard the same story fifty or one hundred times, any positive impact it might have had will have dissipated.

Did you have a happy childhood? Maybe not. Perhaps you suffered through tough times—economically, emotionally, even physically. You may still harbor ill will toward those who helped create your problems. Or perhaps you are angry at God for making your life more difficult than it needed to be. Whatever the issue is, tell the truth about it, reconcile your feelings, and then let it go. Think about St. Julia, who could easily have become embittered over the tragic turn her life took.

Julia was a rich noblewoman who lived in northern Africa in the fifth century and became a victim of the unrest that visited her area. Captured by an enemy army, she was sold into slavery. Fortunately, she was sold to a rich merchant who was suitably impressed with her great beauty and kind manner. He treated her well. When he traveled to Corsica to conduct business with the pagan ruler there, she went with him.

Her master raved about her to the pagan king. Intrigued, the pagan offered the merchant four of his own slave girls for Julia. The merchant refused. However, the pagan ruler was not to be turned down. Behind the merchant's back, he kidnapped Julia. He promised to grant her dream of freedom if only she would denounce Christ. She refused. Infuriated, he had her tortured. Legend has it that her hair was pulled out. After that, in a mockery of her belief in Christ, she was crucified. Today, she is venerated both in Corsica, where she is the patron saint, and in Brescia, Italy, where a magnificent church is dedicated to her.

Julia could easily have become ill-tempered by her precipitous drop in status. After all, she went from being royalty to being a servant. At one time, she had control over her life: where she slept, what she ate, what she did with her days. After she was captured, however, her fate depended upon the whims of others, pagans who loathed her class of people, mocked her beliefs, and felt no guilt over treating her with contempt. Yet we can find no venom in Julia's behavior. Indeed, her kindness helped soften her first master's disposition.

Can you find it in your heart to change your own resentment into acceptance? Is it possible to find some positives in the negative turn your life has taken? Has the adversity made you stronger, wiser, more resourceful? Did a parting of ways lead you to find new relationships that are more nurturing? What uplifting lessons can you bring to your child that will encourage rather than discourage him?

If you truly find that you cannot resolve the issues from your past, then it's time to confront the truth about that stalemate. You need help to put past demons to rest. Start by praying to St. Julia. Ask her to give you a sign that will show you the way.

TEACHING YOUR CHILD
TO BE TRUTHFUL

We all want our children to be truthful in every way. If your child has wounded you with a lie, you know how painful it can be. You cannot understand how your child could fib to you, a mother or father who loves unconditionally. How many times have you uttered the phrase "Just tell me the truth, and I won't punish you"? Still the fabrications tumble forth. When he was a toddler or a small child, you could excuse it. If he broke a toy and refused to own up, you could prod him until he did. You feel as though you did all the right things. What is going on? How could you have failed to teach your child the value of truth?

Draw comfort from this explanation about young adolescent development and lying. Telling the truth is an acquired skill. Conscience begins to emerge around age thirteen. Although a seven-year-old understands right from wrong, it is not until the young adolescent years that a child more deeply comprehends the nuances of behavior, the complexity of truth, and the values that underlie moral decision making and behavior.

In a way, adolescents become judges. They constantly levy verdicts of "It's not fair!" and "Guilty!" even as they themselves are rarely guilty. One of their greatest pleasures is to catch a parent fibbing. ("You always tell me to say you're not home when grandma calls.") They hold that ammunition in reserve to throw back in your face to justify their dishonesty when caught.

They hate to be caught doing something wrong. Lying provides an escape hatch. It is a way of avoiding responsibility, blame, and punishment. At a time when a young adolescent feels assaulted on all fronts—at home, in the classroom, and among his peers—lying becomes a survival mechanism. If you aren't giving your child the independence he wants and needs, lying may be his way to work around that. If he fears being criticized by his friends, putting a gloss on his stories allows him to move up a few notches on the social ladder.

You probably have spent many years trying to teach your child the value of the truth. Now is the time to double those efforts. Honesty is fundamental to character. Without honesty, there is no trust, and without trust, love will falter. Your child will make a poor friend or romantic partner if she is not trustworthy and honest.

Ask that your efforts be blessed by Blessed Sebastian Valfre, who lived from 1629 to 1710 in Turin, Italy. This saint has become a role model for priests because he helped his parishioners embrace Christ. His greatest talent, however, was displayed in the confessional. He was a master at encouraging people to look inward, to recognize their shortcomings and sins. It was said that he was particularly adept at working with soldiers and criminals, probing their souls and compelling them to become introspective and objective about their actions.

One of his secrets was that he was compassionate. We are all sinners, and Blessed Sebastian Valfre did not place himself above others. He did not judge. Ask him for guidance before approaching your child. Implore him to bring to your lips the words that will penetrate the heart of your son or daughter. Set a good example, as Blessed Sebastian Valfre did. Practice what you preach. When you are caught in a lie by your child, own up and apologize. If your child is caught breaking the rules, give him less of a punishment because he told the truth, and be sure to tell him that.

HELPING YOUR CHILD
ACCEPT THE TRUTH

You may already know that your child is in trouble and needs help. After much soul-searching and many gut-wrenching talks with your parenting partner, you both have concluded that you need to take action. You may even have discussed various options. Relatives, friends, and professionals are ready to help you execute your plan. Yet you are frozen. Why? Your child is resisting your every move. You believe that without your child's cooperation, even the best strategy will fail. What do you do? Can you hope to convince your child that something must be done? Should you sit and wait for a sign from him that he is ready to cooperate? How do you quiet the doubts in your mind? Perhaps your child is right when he says he is okay and will figure out on his own what to do. Where do you go from here?

Begin by trusting your instincts. You know your child better than anyone. Listen to this mother who posted on our boards:

> We are having a real problem with our fifteen-year-old daughter. She has been cutting classes at school to be with friends we don't approve of. Last week, she ran away from home for the third time. We are beginning to suspect drug use. This has been going on for almost two years. She says that it is our problem, not hers, that she is doing nothing wrong. She says we should just leave her alone, and everything will be fine. We're not so sure.

Red flags pop up throughout this mother's statement. Chances are that after she reread her missive, even she realized that her daughter was lying. How difficult that revelation must be for any parent. In such situations, the person you love deeply, your child, becomes an adversary. You need to help your child against her will even as you know that she will be angry and condemn you for your actions. Here we are talking about serious measures, moves you are now considering because everything else has failed. Such a move might involve checking your child into a rehabilitation facility, a hospital's psychiatric unit, an eating-disorder center, or perhaps a wilderness therapy program. Whatever the options on your list, you know you will need tremendous strength, resolve, and courage to carry your plan through. There is no tougher trial in parenting. It's time for truth or dare. You know the truth. Dare you take the drastic measures you are contemplating?

Pray to Blessed Kateri Tekakwitha for bravery. This young woman lived a short life that was remarkable for its intense suffering. Some of this misery Kateri endured at the hands of others. However, much of her pain came from her own hand. She wanted to endure the agony for God. We now recognize Kateri's self-inflicted torment as misguided. Yet we cannot condemn her motives. She loved Christ with such devotion that she wanted to share in his distress.

Kateri's father was a Mohawk chief in the Iroquois confederacy, although her mother, an Algonquin, had become a Christian. Born in 1656, Kateri was only four years old when smallpox struck and killed her entire family. Although Kateri was spared, the disease permanently scarred her face and impaired her sight.

In the 1600s, Jesuit missionaries came to upstate New York, where Kateri lived, and attempted to convert the Native Americans to Catholicism. Kateri was enthralled with their teachings, but her uncle, who had taken Kateri in after her parents died, was hostile toward these holy men. Despite her uncle's opposition, she was baptized on Easter Sunday 1676. Thereafter, she was targeted by her own people for turning her back on her Native American beliefs. She fled to a Christian Indian settlement near Montreal on the St. Lawrence River.

Kateri found peace among the people in this religious community, but perhaps she felt she wasn't suffering enough for our Lord. She subjected herself to all types of penance. She fasted, deprived herself of sleep, burned herself, and stayed out in the cold with little protective covering. She and her friend Marie Theresa would scourge each other.

When the Jesuit missionaries became aware of Kateri's humiliations, they ordered her to stop. But no one could question the purity of Kateri's motives. She truly desired to suffer for Christ. The people at the settlement came to call her the "Lily of the Mohawk." Kateri was only twenty-four when she died after a long illness. Her skin remained pockmarked all her life from the smallpox, but after she died, her face was restored to its earlier beauty.

Kateri's brief life was filled with many turning points. Focus on each event as you devise a plan to help your own child.

The death of her parents made Kateri an orphan. Here, contemplate the event that may have triggered your child's turmoil. Chances are, as with Kateri, this event was beyond your control. Remember that fact and try not to blame yourself or others for what has transpired.

Kateri's uncle agreed to take care of her, but from the very beginning he and Kateri faced a major disagreement over religion. If a new adult has entered your household recently, conflict may have followed. Confront this truth and try to find ways to negotiate a compromise between both parties.

Kateri could find no solution to her dilemma within her uncle's home and left to live with the praying community. Perhaps this is the juncture at which you now find yourself. You cannot keep your child safe within your home. That's why you are now contemplating sending your child away. Ask Kateri to guide you as you seek a program that will be worthy of your trust. Implore her to watch over your child, to be with him when you are miles away.

Even at a young age, Kateri recognized that she would find peace, but it would not be found within the community where she had been raised. The same holds true for your child. There will be peace in your child's life again, but his journey to find that calm may take him away from his family for a while. He will not be alone, however. He will have Kateri and our Lord by his side to guide his way. Let their presence in his life comfort you. With the brave Blessed Kateri, he cannot fail to find his way back home.

The Sacrament of Reconciliation

Although God created man and woman in his own image, we are unlike him in our sinfulness. All humans are fallible, including the saintly few who have gone before us or who now walk among us. Ever since Adam and Eve were created, men and women have had lapses in judgment that have resulted in sins against God. However, God never expected humans to be perfect. During his time on earth, Jesus Christ forgave many sinners, but the most powerful message he sent was that those who sought forgiveness would be saved. Tax collectors, beggars, thieves, prostitutes, and others were welcomed into his company after they confessed their sins and repented.

Reflect on forgiveness in your own life. Right now you are probably very angry at your child for the problems he has caused. You might feel as if you will never be in the right frame of mind to accept his apologies for hurting you. You might not want to apologize to him, either, for words you may have spewed out in anger. That's why the sacrament of penance is so important for you at this point in your life. This often-neglected sacrament is Jesus' legacy to us. Penance speaks of forgiveness and second chances. If God can forgive us, we can forgive others.

Jesus' approach toward confession was not a formal one. Throughout the Gospels there are many accounts of Jesus encountering a sinner and forgiving him with simple words: "My child, your sins are forgiven" (to the paralytic at Capernaum); or "Stand up and go on your way. Your faith has saved you" (to the one leper); or "Do not sin any more, or something worse may happen to you" (to the lame man on the Sabbath feast).

Penitential rituals were very much a part of religion during Jesus' time. Among the Jewish people, the Day of Atonement was when the high priest confessed his and other people's sins to God. According to Greg Dues, in *Catholic Customs and Traditions,* the priest then transferred the people's sins to a goat, which was then driven into the wilderness—hence the term *scapegoat.*

Christ did not impose penance on those whose sins he forgave. However, over the centuries, church officials decided that those who had committed grave sins against the church should be required to somehow make restitution before they could be forgiven. In some communities, sinners were banished until they repented, a practice first given credence by St. Paul. In his first letter to the Corinthians, he advised: "You must banish this evil-doer from among you." Grave sins were considered to be murder, idolatry, and adultery. A sinner would have to perform his penance in public, sometimes for years, before he would be welcomed back into the church. Such penance might have included going without meat, wine, sexual relations with a spouse, bathing, or shaving.

According to the *Catechism of the Catholic Church,* seventh-century Irish missionaries who had been influenced by the Eastern monastic tradition came back to Europe and introduced the idea of the private act of penance. In this form, the sinner confessed his sins to the priest and performed his act of contrition away from the public's view. Since that time, the sacrament has been conducted privately, with the penitent confessing his sins to a priest, who then prescribes an appropriate act of penance, usually praying the Hail Mary and the Our Father several times. Catholics view the priest as having assumed the responsibility once bestowed upon the apostles of forgiving sins. Confessing sins to ourselves, even if we do so in church during Mass, is not the same thing as confessing to a priest.

Following the Council of Trent, in the sixteenth century, St. Charles Borromeo designed a confessional similar to the one we are familiar with today, with the confessor's chair boxed in by a screen. In 1614, Greg Dues says, this style of confessional was mandated by the church to assure anonymity and protect women from solicitation. Of course, all penitents are protected by the seal of confession, which forbids a priest to reveal any sin, however grave, told to him during the sacrament of penance. This seal is sacrosanct and has withstood many a legal challenge (and has provided the grist for many a movie plot).

In 1973, the church made some changes in how the sacrament of penance was administered. An alternative was offered to the traditional closed-box confessional. In the new arrangement, the penitent does not kneel but sits in a chair facing the confessor without a screen between them. It was hoped that this new open atmosphere would encourage a freer exchange. Those parishioners who felt they needed counseling along with their absolution were encouraged to make use of this option. These days when new churches are designed, the architects often include several small rooms that can be used as counseling rooms.

Another change was the advent of penitential celebrations, where congregants pray, sing, repent, and ask for God's forgiveness as a community. This ceremony, however, does not have the same force as an individual confession. Each penitent should still visit the confessional to receive absolution.

The church decrees that Catholics should receive penance and communion at least once a year. While most Catholics receive communion more frequently, many tend to steer clear of the confessional. You may be one. That's no surprise. It's no fun admitting your sins to another human, even if this person is a priest bound by church law to guard your secrets. Your childhood memories of a dark, enclosed space where you were dressed down for your minor youthful transgressions might still rankle. Now is a good time to evaluate why you avoid confession and reflect on what this sacrament can bring to your life.

Reconciliation can open your heart. As a parent of a troubled child, you may always feel as if you are being sinned against. Going to confession can help remind you that we all make mistakes. If God can forgive you, how can you withhold your forgiveness from others, particularly your child?

Confession can bring home the power of truth. You may preach to your child about telling the truth, but facing a priest and having to tell the truth yourself will help you empathize with your child. Telling the truth is sometimes difficult. Can you be as sympathetic and forgiving with your child as the priest and God are with you?

The new counseling rooms can help you seek help for yourself and your child. Because the new open confessional encourages conversation, you can tell the priest not only about your sins, but also about your struggles with your child. Chances are that besides absolving you, he will offer to help you in other ways, possibly by putting you in touch with resources in your community.

Penance can bring you and your child together. With the right timing, you might be able to encourage your child to attend a penance service with you. Worshiping together and asking for God's help in forgiving each other may be the jump start you have been looking for.

Receiving the sacrament of reconciliation can mark the beginning of a new attitude in your family, an attitude that favors truth over lying, forgiveness over resentment, and peace over discord. Penance can remind us that sometimes revealing the truth will be painful, but some discomfort is necessary before the healing process can begin. With the saints whose lives we have explored in this chapter, we can pray that by opting for the truth in all aspects of our lives, we can bring our family closer together and, at the same time, move closer to God.

Prayer for Truth

Dear St. Agnes, you were just a young girl when you were put to the test. Yet despite the agonies you faced, you were unafraid to tell the truth. Help me cope with the unpleasant truths in my life. St. Dorothy, through your example, I will try to become a better role model for my child. Whenever I falter, be there by my side to remind me of your presence, just as the angel reminded Theophilus with your apples and roses. St. Julia, you never resented others for the unpleasant turn your life took. Too often I blame others, especially my own child, for my misery. Restore my spirit so that I can avoid blaming others for my situation. Blessed Kateri, what courage it must have taken to leave your people because of your beliefs. Help me stand by my convictions so that I can aid my child. Blessed Sebastian Valfre, with your guidance I will rediscover the sacrament of reconciliation. My truthful confession will mark a new beginning for me and my family. Amen.

Saints Who Can Help You Seek Truth

St. Agnes can give you courage to confront the truth.

St. Dorothy can inspire you to be a truthful role model.

St. Julia can help you accept the truth without bitterness.

Blessed Sebastian Valfre can show you how to make a good confession.

Blessed Kateri Tekakwitha can guide you to a plan to save your child.

Discussion Questions

1. One lie leads to another, and even a small fib can be hurtful. If you are lecturing your child about lying, remember to monitor your own actions. Are there some occasions when you feel justified in lying? If you get caught lying, how could that affect your child's behavior?

2. Like Blessed Sebastian Valfre, be compassionate. Your child may not know why he is lying, cheating, stealing, or sneaking out. Let your child know that you value truth above all else. If your child breaks a rule but fesses up, can you impose a lesser penalty?

3. Sometimes we choose to ignore the obvious—a child using drugs, breaking curfew, stealing—because we dread disturbing the harmony in our home. Yet the problem won't go away on its own and may even reach crisis proportions. What support do you need so that you can confront the truth about your child?

4. Embarrassment over your child's actions may prevent you from being truthful to others. Identify your fears (loss of friends, damage to your image, condemnation of your child by others). Are these fears realistic? Is it possible that people might be more understanding than you think?

5. Are you hiding the truth about your own turbulent adolescence? You may not want to share all the details with your child, but at least be truthful with yourself. Could guilt over your own behavior be hampering your ability to parent? Would going to confession and talking about your past transgressions help you wipe the slate clean?

6. St. Dorothy found worthy role models in her parents, who, admittedly, were nearly perfect. Even imperfect parents, however, can inspire their children. Think about ways you can set a good example for your child. Remember that your actions speak louder than words.

7. St. Julia could have railed against her captors, but she adjusted to her situation and managed to be good-natured. How often have you taken out your anger over your child on someone who did nothing to deserve your wrath? Is it time to mend some fences? Tell the truth about why you lashed out. Resolve to find less hurtful ways (punching a pillow, perhaps) to deal with your anger.

8. Blessed Kateri Tekakwitha subjected herself to physical pain to please the Lord. While her intentions were pure, we recognize today that her methods were misguided. Is your child hurting herself—through cutting, for example—in an attempt to feel better? If you have been overlooking warning signs, is it time for you to seek professional aid for her?

9. You know the truth: your child needs more help than you can give. How do you convince your child of this truth without risking an outright rebellion? Would family and friends participate in an intervention? Would a school professional offer a workable strategy? Come up with a plan before you sit down with your child.

10. In the short term, facing the truth about your child will be hard. How can you deal with your doubts on a daily basis so that your resolve isn't weakened? Whom can you lean on for fortification?

chapter eight

Humility

Love is not to be purchased,
and affection has no price.

—St. Jerome

The cornerstone of American culture is success. Riches, celebrity, accomplishment, status—these are what drive individuals to pursue the American dream. Getting humility, or displaying it, isn't the national pastime. Our world and our fantasies revolve around "me" and around the lives of megacelebrities and megamillionaires. Humility isn't in vogue. Nor does it come naturally or easily.

On top of that simple truth, our world tantalizes us with the promise of having it all—"it" being wealth, good health, beauty, and even eternal youth. Business gurus travel around spouting formulas for amassing a fast fortune with a product or a service. Health experts write books urging cancer patients to think positively and laugh heartily, and a cure will be at hand. Everything is cast as accessible to us.

And so many of us religiously hunt out the expertise, heed the advice, educate ourselves, and work hard to acquire those fruits of our labor.

Yet even the most gifted and most successful among us can find ourselves in dire straights with our adolescents. Many parents look in the mirror and ponder, *How could I have a child like this?* Locked in family trauma, they cry out loud or think silently, "It's not fair!"

Are you familiar with the old saying "When you walk down the street, you are a reflection of me"? It's the kind of adage that comes out of your mouth involuntarily. As you mouth the words you think to yourself: *I'm turning into my mother [father].* That saying was true for our parents, and it rings true for us now that we are parents. An adolescent who goes off track or hits the bottom is a reflection of us, and an embarrassment. It is normal for a conscientious parent (yes, you) to feel that such a turn of events isn't fair. After all, haven't you tried to do the right thing in the parenting department for more than a decade? Haven't you made the sacrifices required?

For the time being, retire such questions. Put aside the public image that you wear in your everyday world. Put your private outrage on hold, too. What's important now is not your image but your child's. Neither your pride nor your wounded pride helps a troubled child.

In this chapter, we will question your current standards for measuring yourself. We will transform how you look at yourself, your ambitions, and the ordinary tasks you perform. In the process, expect your values to be turned upside down and inside out. We offer you the ironic truth that humility will give you perspective on your ordeals and even give them meaning. Humility can change the way you deal with your teenager. We'll explore the boundaries between fault and chance, between self-esteem and arrogance. We will come to know the humble hearts of saints who excelled at humility, from St. Margaret Mary Alacoque to St. Katharine Drexel, and we will show you how to cultivate humility with community service.

WHY YOU? WHY NOT YOU?

When we meet parents throughout the country at our talks or during our online chats, we frequently hear outbursts like this one:

My thirteen-year-old boy, a seventh grader, is free-falling. Until last year, he was an A/B student. I've been receiving calls from teachers left and right this year because he is failing nearly every subject. They tell me that he doesn't do homework and rushes carelessly through class work. Several of his teachers implied he may be using drugs. My husband and I have taken away every privilege: video games, PC, TV, CD Walkman, MTV—to no avail. He just sits in his room. We have stooped to searching that room and the backpack in it. I thought behavior like this happened because of divorce or bad parents. My husband and I are good, hardworking role models. We are two working parents, both here every evening, with a stable home life. We are at a loss.

If truth be told, there is no way to ensure against having a child who makes mistakes, even big ones. A brilliant pair of physicians who as teens had nothing but determination can sire a ne'er-do-well with absolutely no work ethic. Teachers do find themselves parenting an underachiever who talks back to his teachers and threatens to drop out of high school. In the war between parents and their young adolescents, a child knows exactly which button to push to irritate parents and exactly how to fail a parent in the most hurtful way. Even though we can and do affect the path our children take and continue on, we are not always responsible. We are not necessarily to blame.

When it comes to the adversity placed in our path as parents, we don't always get what we deserve.

Right here and now, get rid of that "It's not fair" or that "Why me?" attitude. Don't waste one more second lying prostrate, looking toward the Almighty, and bemoaning your being singled out for an undeserved trial. You are hardly alone as the parent of a difficult adolescent.

Consider this: in a 1999 Institute of Medicine report on adolescents, it was estimated that approximately one-quarter of teenagers are at risk for either psychological or social problems, specifically drinking, drug use, academic failure, and run-ins with the law. Realize how many other mothers and fathers, stepparents and grandparents—one out of four—are in this same rocking boat.

Stepparents are particularly vulnerable, says Dr. James Bray, expert and coauthor of *Stepfamilies: Love, Marriage, and Parenting in the First Decade,* who conducted a nine-year study of these hybrid families that was sponsored by the National Institutes of Health. Their poor odds amount to this: 20 percent of children living in stepfamilies have behavior problems, compared to 10 percent in traditional families. It is during early adolescence that these battles surface. This pattern holds even in those stepfamilies that have overcome the rough patches in the beginning and have been running smoothly for five years.

Here is one example:

> *My fifteen-year-old stepson has been stealing from our home. Each time he's here for visitation, something else turns up missing, small stuff to costly items. Last time my wedding rings disappeared. We canceled visitation after that for two months. His mom is no help. She sends him to his room, which has a TV, sound system,*

*and computer. Not much punishment there! And to top
it off, then he doesn't have to babysit his younger siblings. I assign chores, but he refuses to do them. His
father, my husband, doesn't correct him. He feels guilty
about the divorce. He's afraid of the ex taking him back
to court. Very sad. So I am alone in all this. I don't see
things changing with two—what can I say?—wishy-
washy parents.*

Stepmothers and stepfathers often feel they are "better"
than biological parents. Ex-spouses can be guilt-ridden, pre-
occupied, or just plain negligent. Post-divorce emotions and
actions can hamper their parenting. A stepparent's feelings
of superiority may be based in fact, and yet therein lies
the danger of arrogance. Even if you, the stepmother, are a
more efficient caregiver, are you implicitly putting down a
stepchild's parents? Children of divorce are loyal to their
parents, whether they should be or not. They are delicate and
explosive. Parenting such teenagers is complicated even in
the best of stepfamilies.

Whether you are a step- or traditional parent, holding
yourself up too often as a paragon of achievement and wisdom
has drawbacks. Comparing yourself to a teenager who is bent
on self-destruction (or having a teen make the comparison himself) widens the distance between you. As you go about prov-
ing yourself as an impeccable role model, you risk alienating
even further a child who sees himself as a black sheep or the
family failure. Putting down the other parent or an absentee
ex-spouse, even if it's justified, backfires. It makes the child
defend his or her parent more and move further into that
hostile camp. It ensures that you will be rejected along with
your well-intended and even wise guidance.

A New Standard for Measuring

God hasn't always designated the best and the brightest to be parents—quite the contrary. Look at whom God the Father chose to raise his only Son, Jesus. He could have picked a king and an empress—a couple like Cleopatra and Marc Antony—or a genius like Galileo. Instead he settled upon simple people, Joseph and Mary, whom you have met in earlier chapters. Their qualifications were anything but showy. They were humble, hardworking, and good citizens.

Joseph and Mary became God's chosen parents for Jesus. Did that guarantee smooth sailing? No, indeed. Joseph and Mary struggled, too, with a man-child who went against the grain. Jesus was a declared misfit, a revolutionary, and was crucified for not upholding the status quo. If you have wept many tears for your child, all the while feeling your plight isn't fair, think of how many tears Mary wept. Ponder how Joseph felt about a Son who didn't want to follow in his footsteps but followed a new path.

Like Father, like Son, Jesus also made surprising choices when he gathered his apostles. He didn't collect his followers from the club of Hebrew highbrows and holy men, the Pharisees. He recruited fishermen. He even reached out to a tax collector, Matthew, a Jew of Galilee who worked for Rome.

Throughout history, tax collectors have never been popular. In American history, we have the colonists spitting in the face of King George III, the supreme tax man. Think Boston Tea Party and its battle cry, "No taxation without representation." The Jews at the time of Jesus couldn't stand these publicans either. Tax collectors were avoided as much as possible and excluded from religious and community events.

In this context, Jesus' recruiting of a dreaded tax man was surprising. Jesus' visit to Matthew's office in Capernaum and his command, "Follow me," certainly raised eyebrows and probably caused disbelief, too. The next thing Jesus did was go to dinner at Matthew's, where the guest list included all men of a similar background. Jesus reached out to these powerful men who were considered spiritually bankrupt. By instructing Matthew to leave his old life behind, a life of fiscal expertise and power, and take up a new calling, Jesus implied that the status quo paled in comparison to the life he offered. Jesus offered a new blueprint for salvation.

We can draw this conclusion: men who are part of the establishment, with wealth and clout on their side, are not necessarily men to be emulated. Jesus personified new values and revealed a new standard of spiritual work and nonmaterial rewards.

Matthew followed Jesus through his Savior's death and resurrection. Then he wrote the first Gospel, originally intended for Jewish converts to Christianity. In Matthew's version, the themes of humility and simple values come up again and again. While Jesus walked this earth, he was very clear on these subjects. If you review the Sermon on the Mount, you will hear his best words about them, the Beatitudes:

> How blessed are the poor in spirit:
> the kingdom of Heaven is theirs.
> Blessed are the gentle:
> they shall have the earth as inheritance.
> Blessed are those who mourn:
> they shall be comforted.
> Blessed are those who hunger and thirst for uprightness:
> they shall have their fill.

Blessed are the merciful:
they shall have mercy shown them.
Blessed are the pure in heart:
they shall see God.
Blessed are the peacemakers:
they shall be recognized as children of God.
Blessed are those who are persecuted in the cause of
    uprightness:
the kingdom of Heaven is theirs. (Matthew 5:3–10)

Throughout Matthew's Gospel we hear the message that the proudest will be humbled. We are not suggesting that you do what Matthew did—quit your job and leave your home— but we are recommending that you consider how much of your time and energy you have invested in maintaining the status quo. When you calculate your worth according to your professional success and your social standing, you tend to see your children as either contributing to your public image or tarnishing it. In that equation, you are at the center, not your child.

If you pride yourself on your ambition, your achievements, your beautiful home, and your fashionable wardrobe, you will find it even harder to love a child who thumbs her nose at those things. When your child fails at or rebels against the philosophy that guides your life, it will cause you deep pain. If you are a business self-starter, you will chafe at your son's lack of effort and failing grades. If you work hard to create a *Better Homes and Gardens* decor, your daughter's sloppy room will send you over the edge.

If you change your course, leaving behind your material world and professional route and focusing on humility and spiritual issues, you will have a new agenda and a new approach to your relationship with yourself, with God, and with your child. Rather than spending your time wringing your hands over poor report cards and your child's earrings, think about his heart and soul. After all, isn't that most important?

It's hard to shift gears like this when everywhere you look people are talking about remodeling their homes, shopping for designer fashions, buying newer automobiles, and planning their Las Vegas vacations. The fact that you are reading this book proves you have made a significant step toward balancing your life with more spiritual resources. As you simplify your life and your standards, you will see your child in a whole new light.

A Look at the Heart of Humility

Humility takes work. Others might not understand your motives and might even ridicule you. That is what happened to Margaret Mary Alacoque. A look at her life can help you on this difficult path.

Margaret's life story isn't one of those riches-to-rags tales about a saint who leaves behind family fortune and an impressive family name. No, Margaret's path to sainthood began when she was already in humble circumstances. At the age of twenty-four, Margaret entered the Visitation convent in the French town of Paray-le-Monial. Margaret was not outstanding but was thought of as somewhat clumsy and even slow.

Two days after Christmas 1673, Margaret was praying in the convent chapel at night when she had a vision of Jesus. She described what happened next: "He [Jesus] made me lean on his divine breast, while He revealed to me the marvels of His love and the inexplicable secrets of His Sacred Heart. I am always afraid of deceiving myself about what I say has taken place within me. But the results that this grace produced in me made me sure."

Jesus confided to Margaret an entirely new devotion, a devotion to his Sacred Heart, which he wanted her to explain to everyone. He revealed the exact way that he wanted the heart to be illustrated, namely, as a human heart surrounded by a crown of thorns. Jesus asked Margaret to make sure his Sacred Heart was produced in picture form and assured her that those who displayed it would receive many graces.

Jesus appeared again and again to Margaret over an eighteen-month period and mapped out the exact steps that the devotion should take: people should attend Mass and take communion on the first Friday of each month for nine months. On the Thursday night before, one hour should be spent meditating on the image of the Sacred Heart. He explained to Margaret that this time would be in commemoration of his night in the Garden of Gethsemane, where he contemplated his final hours on earth.

Jesus also announced that he wanted a new feast day established in honor of the Sacred Heart and scheduled into the Catholic calendar. Margaret accepted Jesus' presence in her life and carefully recorded all his holy orders to her.

Margaret felt confident about the instructions she got directly from our Lord Jesus Christ. Her mother superior, however, was not so confident. She doubted Margaret's tale and judged her to be delusional. Rather than follow through with the devotion to the Sacred Heart that Margaret explained, her fellow nuns just dismissed her as what we would now call a nutcase. As she was facing this ridicule and rejection, Jesus told her that he would send her a little help.

On the scene came a new confessor by the name of Claude de La Colombiere, who became Margaret's ally and supporter.

Now at least she had one person who treated her kindly while those in her sisterhood did not. Margaret's superior came round slowly. At one point she told a seriously ailing Margaret that if she recovered quickly it would be a sign that she was telling the truth. Margaret did indeed get well overnight, and that was the beginning of others believing that this humble and ordinary sister could actually be a messenger for Christ.

Margaret's visions of Jesus as the Sacred Heart were never sanctioned. She didn't become an instant heroine. No, Margaret continued her life quietly and without fanfare in her convent. Eventually, the devotion was practiced in her convent, and the community of sisters erected a chapel dedicated to the Sacred Heart. Other convents followed suit, and with the passing of time the Sacred Heart of Jesus devotion spread throughout the Catholic world. In 1690, Margaret died. In 1920, 230 years later, she was canonized for her vision and her visionary role in Catholic history and tradition.

Margaret apparently never looked for the fame she now has. On her deathbed, she whispered, "I need nothing but God, and to lose myself in the heart of Jesus."

Margaret was not made a doctor of the church, or the focus of shrines in her own lifetime, but she knew that outside recognition wasn't important. Her communion with Jesus, experienced in the quiet of her chapel, was what counted. She wasn't wrapped up in winning people's adulation for being singled out by God. Her humility served her well and kept her focus on Jesus. It sustained her through supernatural melodrama and public humiliation. Margaret knew that her sanctity and purity of soul were all she needed.

From Margaret's example, you can learn that you need to let go of the opinion of others. Let them have their say. Forget about all the trappings of fame and ambition. Instead get down to basics and measure yourself against the standard of your spiritual well-being.

A Unique Vision of Aspirations

Central to Margaret's experience were her visions of Jesus. These apparitions became the touchstone of her actions and aspirations. Her spiritual sensations became so powerful, so incredibly rewarding and strengthening, that she needed nothing more to feel fulfilled.

You may be thinking that rapture was easy for her because she didn't have a belligerent teenager bent on self-destruction interrupting her peace. That may be true. It is time, however, for you to get in touch with what Margaret touched—the hand of God, not just figuratively, but literally.

Try totally changing your goals, at least temporarily, directing them toward God. Think for a moment about your present aspirations. Do you want to impress your boss, stir envy in your neighbor with that new pond you dug in your backyard, dazzle your friends with your new look? Add your own goal. On a scale of one to ten, rate just how significant these outward, materialistic goals are to your self-image. Be honest.

Now spend a moment gauging how important it is to you what people think and say about your child. If your child isn't living up to your values, consider this plea of a mother who told us that she has spent a lifetime practicing modesty, good taste, and social restraint but now faces a daughter who has taken another path:

> *I need help with my fifteen-year-old daughter. She has had more sexual partners than I have had in my entire*

life. People don't say it to my face, but I know what
everyone is calling her. When I try to tell her what kind
of a reputation she is getting, she gets argumentative.
What am I going to do? How could I have raised a girl
who is so far from my ideals?

You may not realize how this way of thinking affects your
teenager. If the social pecking order and others' judgments are
uppermost in your mind, and if your child falls short of or is
an embarrassment in light of those judgments, she knows it.
The more ashamed you are of your child, the more shame your
child carries with her every day. Make no mistake about it: she
feels worthless—whether you scold her or not.

That is the best reason to change your way of thinking.
Introduce yourself to a new aspiration: feeling God's hand in
your life.

Wait a minute. Can you actually feel God's hand in your
life? Isn't that expectation arrogant with a capital *A*? Not at all.
Catholic tradition is filled with stories of ordinary human
beings who met God personally in their dreams and reveries.
You have read some of those stories in this book. Each of us is
loved and tended to by God our Father. Each of us will be able
to know the wisdom of the Holy Spirit if we tune in to him.
You—all of us—are just as qualified as Margaret or Augustine,
Bernadette of Lourdes or Benedict to feel God's presence. We
don't have to be saints in the making to see God or hear God's
voice in our life. Each of us is worthy.

According to Eddie Ensley, a Native American and Roman
Catholic theologian who has spent forty years studying visions,
experiencing God in a personal way or seeing signs of him is no
longer an ordinary occurrence, and this is unfortunate.
Nowadays when we think of those people who have visions,

our mind conjures up schizophrenic kooks or delusional pilgrims having paranormal episodes at crowded shrines.

In his book *Visions: The Soul's Path to the Sacred,* Ensley explains how the Catholic Church downplayed this sacred aspect of spirituality and why:

> *Several centuries ago, church and society stopped talking about visions and wonder. Many thinkers turned away and grew ashamed of the Western religion's long history of wonder. Visions still happened. Miracles still brought people to awe, but opinion makers—the philosophers, and writers, even the theologians—grew ashamed of these stories. Tales of the holy were generally banished from educated discussion.*

The rise of a scientific perspective resulted in the dismissal of anything that could not be explained empirically. Having extraordinary rapport with God, though, is in our Catholic tradition and is our religious birthright. Raised on the vision stories of his Cherokee grandfather and now a student of the rich tradition of visions in our Catholic history, Ensley is convinced that we should be open to reconnecting with God in our thoughts and dreams. He reminds us, "Visions are a combination of sacred touch and inner response. The touches of God are beyond the telling. The telling comes from within us. Visions can transform, heal, and brighten our lives."

Concentrate on what's inside you, not on outside characteristics. Commit to enriching your one-on-one rapport with God. Listen for God's encouragement or guidance. In the same way, commit to nurturing a one-on-one relationship with your child—without the cloud of public opinion or personal embarrassment hanging over you.

St. Katharine: From the Good Life to God's Life

A useful exercise to help you cultivate humility is to concentrate on moving Godward rather than upward or forward. Our Roman Catholic tradition is littered with legendary tales of saints who did just that—gave up social stature, family name, and wealth to live a spare and hermitlike existence. Remember St. Alphonsus and St. Benedict? While such pious makeover stories are dramatic and telling, they often lack relevance to our modern life. Perhaps that is why the pope recently canonized St. Katharine Drexel.

Katharine was a banker's daughter, born in 1858. As with many upper-class families, philanthropy was a family value for the Drexels. Katharine's stepmother trained her and her sisters well and guided them into community programs that provided food, clothing, medicine, and rent money to impoverished families of their day.

Then, in 1883, Katharine's stepmother died. Her father died two years later. Left behind was a fourteen-million-dollar estate. Katharine's income was considerable, to say the least. She could have lived like other heiresses. She could have become a big-name donor and attended charity benefits and gala fund-raisers. Like many in that philanthropic circle, she could have enjoyed the best things in life, including dining in fine restaurants, wearing the best clothes, and vacationing at the most elite hideaways all around the globe.

Instead, Katharine began donating thousands to the Bureau of Catholic Indian Missions for the construction of Native American schools. On a European trip, she met Pope Leo XIII and asked him to send more missionaries to help Native Americans and blacks. He responded by suggesting Katharine become the missionary she was lobbying for. And that is exactly how her life unfolded.

Katharine the socialite became a nun and founded a new religious community called the Sisters of the Blessed Sacrament for Indians and Colored People, an order that combined prayer and social action. Katharine and her sisters, financed by the revenue of her fourteen-million-dollar fortune, built 145 Catholic missions, 12 schools for Native American children, and 50 schools for blacks. Katharine founded Xavier University in New Orleans in 1915, the first university for African Americans in the United States.

It's hard to imagine giving away an entire fortune, isn't it? Even harder to comprehend is forgoing all the worldly thrills, adventures, perks, and pleasures. Could you do that? Could we? How did Katharine manage?

She explains herself in these words:

> *European travel brings vividly before the mind how cities have risen and fallen; and the same of empires and kingdoms and nations. And the billions and billions who have lived their common everyday life in these nations and kingdoms and empires and cities, where are they? The ashes of the kings and mighty of this earth are mingled with the dust of the meanest slave.*
>
> *The question alone important, the solution of which depends upon how I have spent my life, is the state of my soul at the moment of my death. And the question for me is to be decided at most in seventy years, seventy short years compared with eternity.*

Despite her fortunate birthright, Katharine had the highest sense of priorities and the clearest vision of what is most important in this life: one's soul. With that perspective, she found using her wealth for spiritual health to be a simple foregone conclusion. The high life or good life didn't hold any allure for her. Katharine gladly paid the highest price for her humility because she had the most to spend.

CORPORAL WORKS OF MERCY

No matter where you fall on the ladder of life, economically or socially, you, too, can find humility and meaning in the service of others. How can you do that?

In our younger days when we memorized catechism questions and answers, doing good works was called performing "spiritual and corporal works of mercy." In today's parlance that would be doing some form of community service. Spending time at a soup kitchen making peanut-butter-and-jelly sandwiches for the homeless, joining a hospital staff to read to sick children, holding AIDS babies or chatting with elderly patients in an urban hospital ward, planting a community vegetable patch, or hammering nails for a Habitat for Humanity house— the variety of possibilities is staggering.

Once you commit to volunteering, how do you decide what effort is right for you? Where do you begin? You can go the easiest route and look within your community. Most parishes have any number of programs designed to help the less-affluent members of the community. Many parish members run thrift shops, food banks, day-care centers, visitation programs to the elderly, and more. You can also inquire about opportunities at your local hospitals or nursing-care facilities.

Schools also have volunteer prospects, but for you they may not be a good option. If your child has become known as a troublemaker or problem child, that reputation and a bias against your family may get in the way of your participation. You are better off turning to neutral territory.

When zeroing in on a volunteer project, make sure that you choose work that interests you. A good fit will ensure that you stay motivated. If you love books, for instance, work for a literacy campaign. It won't seem like work, and it will be rewarding to share your love of literature by teaching someone to embrace reading. On the flip side, if you have a soft heart and a weak stomach, the pediatrics department of a hospital might not be the right choice. You won't be able to handle facing the specter of children who are afflicted with fatal diseases or who were the victims of tragedies like automobile accidents.

If the usual volunteer opportunities fail to interest you or you don't find anything satisfactory in your hometown, the Internet is a wonderful, cutting-edge resource for locating volunteer programs. For example, Volunteer Match (www.volunteer match.org) is a nonprofit volunteer-matching database that helps people find activities in their area of interest within five to sixty miles of their ZIP code. Does putting together a talent show with inner-city teens interest you? If you are fluent in another language, why not help recent immigrants translate paperwork? These are but a few examples of what you might find.

Would you consider combining travel with volunteering? If so, clicking onto Idealist (www.idealist.org) will bring you to a world of possibilities, quite literally. This site contains a volunteer-matching database that includes 18,000 nonprofit organizations in 130 countries. Apparently, the Internet is a godsend for organizations looking to recruit talented and committed volunteers both nationally and overseas. It can also be a godsend for you, pointing you in the right direction.

Volunteering to help those in need changes your perspective. You may start out eager to share your love of books. The emphasis is on your motivation and your passion. Soon, though, you will become focused on the youngster you are tutoring. He might never have had the stable family life to allow him to concentrate on learning. An older illiterate adult with whom you work might have had to drop out of school early in order to support her family and may still be working hard, with little to show for the effort. Your selfishness will slip away as you recognize the determination, valiance, and needs of others. You will probably come to the realization that their burdens are far greater than yours. You will find your pride shrink in the process; your compassion will grow to fill that space. Never again will you feel with quite the same conviction that you are alone or singled out for hardship.

Not only is community service valuable for you and your spiritual growth, but it can be rewarding for your troubled adolescent, too. This mother's testimonial makes that point:

> *I pray every day for the children and the parents of this country! It is so hard to raise a child in this era. Once upon a time, kids went to work at the age of twelve and were kept busy. Now you have to invent things to keep them entertained, starting around thirteen until they can finally get a job at fifteen or sixteen. They are easily bored since they are raised on Nintendo and TV. If things aren't running ninety miles an hour, they seem to be sitting still.*
>
> *When my son hit fifth grade, we ran into problems. He was hanging around too much with friends I didn't trust and got into some minor trouble with vandalism. With summer on the horizon and me working, I knew I*

*needed a plan. So I called a local retirement home to see
if my son could go there and volunteer once or twice a
week for the summer. The first question out of the direc-
tor's mouth: "Why? Does he have to do community
service?" I reassured this person that my son was not a
juvenile offender with such a sentence, and so he agreed.
Well, as it turned out, my son spent EVERY day there,
he loved it so much. They loved him, too. I know he will
always remember those afternoons playing checkers,
doing wheelchair wheelies on the grounds, and listening
to old stories (American history, really) from those
grandmas and grandpas.*

Volunteering can give a teenager a clean slate. It is a second chance to do something meaningful, and do it well. Just
as community service can turn your way of looking at things
upside down, it can also shift your troubled child's perspective. The teenager who feels like a failure sees himself anew in
the eyes of appreciative children and adults. He will realize
that he has the personal power to light up the lives of others.
He can and does make a difference. No child can help but
benefit from that discovery and the glow reflected back from
others. This process can go a long way toward changing the
self-image of a troubled teen.

It is arrogant for parents to believe that we are the best
people to help our children in their distress. Sometimes that
simply isn't the case. It is humbling to face the fact that there
are times when strangers can be more influential than we are.

If you want to help your adolescent find a way to donate
his time, the organization to contact is Youth Service America.
In the spring of 2000, their National Youth Service Day had
more than three million young people and adults working on

more than ten thousand projects. For more information, call 1-800-VOLUNTEER or visit their Web site at www.SERVEnet .org. Teens can access specific listings by ZIP code, too.

Corporal works of mercy move us away from professional agendas, social pecking orders, and materialistic feeding frenzies. On the spiritual ladder, the "stepping up" of humility takes us to another world. Cultivating humility involves changing. We have to let go of our usual notions and try a new course. The only worthwhile currency is spiritual. Humility can save us and our families. As you and your child do some meaningful service for others, you both will feel a bonus.

In the end, practicing humility will have an unforeseen result. As you whittle down your pride, as you rid yourself of those martyrlike feelings of being put upon by your child, your embarrassment over your situation will dwindle. As your vision becomes less self-centered, you will be able to see your child differently. Without the shadow of others' opinions, you will be in a new relationship with your son or daughter. You will find a new sensitivity and ability to appreciate her struggle, her pain, her crippled self-image, and her burden. Then you will be able to be of service to the person who matters most to you: your child. With a greater commitment to spiritual values, you will have a simpler measure for your child and yourself: your souls.

Prayer for Humility

> Dear God, I promise you here and now that I am going to work on turning my pride into something more useful. My ego, my bank account, my worries about what others think of me—none of these are

worthy of my thoughts now. Instead I will turn my attention to you and to those whose needs are greater than my own. Let me become an instrument to help others prosper spiritually. I shall work to replace my materialistic agenda with a spiritual one. When worldly goods and social opinions entice me, I will turn to St. Margaret Mary Alacoque and to St. Katharine Drexel to remind me that what counts is my commitment to you. Shave my consciousness until all that remains is the vision of you and me. As our one-on-one relationship intensifies, keep that vision of my soul in my eyes. Guide me to sacred places and humble hearts until I am brimming with compassion for others. If I struggle to simplify myself, reward me by showering me with your grace until I am worthy of being the parent my child needs. Amen.

Saints Who Can Guide You toward Humility

St. Joseph and St. Mary can serve as role models and keep you aware that simple people make wonderful parents.

St. Matthew can remind you that the status quo is not the most important measure.

St. Margaret Mary Alacoque can inspire you to ignore the opinions of others and look only to God for validation.

St. Katharine Drexel can help you realize the importance of community service and of placing the soul above all else.

Discussion Questions

1. Most of us have our own version of the American dream toward which we strive. What drives you? Accomplishment? Fame? Fortune? If you were to create a pie of your aspirations, what portion of it would be dedicated to your spiritual goals?

2. In our culture, it's hard to get away from status-oriented thinking. Which schools we want our children to attend, what neighborhood we want to live in, which group of friends we socialize with—the desire to move upward prevails, even in the world of religion. How often do you pat yourself on the back for being Catholic, on the fast lane to heaven, more enlightened than your Pentecostal, Protestant, or Jewish counterparts?

3. "When you walk down the street, you are a reflection of me." This saying often tumbles from the mouths of parents looking to jump-start a child to shape up. Reflect on this for a moment. Would your parents, would God the Father, be proud of you? Proud of who you are, not merely what you do or what you have? How so?

4. Does your son or daughter, your stepson or stepdaughter embarrass you? Do you think that your child is aware of the shame you feel? Has he ever articulated this burden of shame that you have placed on his shoulders?

5. Ironically, children often fail us in exactly the most devastating way. A modest mother has a promiscuous siren as a daughter; a pillar of the community has raised the town flake; a brilliant professional is faced with an underachieving dropout of a son. The lives of the saints—for example, St. Francis of Assisi— demonstrate this pattern as well. Discuss why and how this happens. Is it a coincidence?

6. Do you hold your child to a timetable? Do you give her six months to stop smoking or two months to bring her grades up? St. Margaret Mary Alacoque had no use for timetables. She never cared that her community didn't recognize her immediately, in a year, or in her lifetime for being singled out by God to reveal the devotion to the Sacred Heart. "I need nothing but God" was her mantra. Does God have a timetable for us?

7. St. Margaret had the ability to remain oblivious to the opinion of others. How can you let go of being concerned about what others say, think, or feel about you or your troubled child? Can you target gossip as an issue in your life and your family's life and work toward eliminating it in conversation? How?

8. Do you feel God's love touching you occasionally? Do you hear God's voice of consolation and reassurance from time to time? If the answer is no, could it be that you need to strip away some of the activities, commitments, chores, and deadlines that absorb you?

9. Many parents, like us, can't stop giving advice. We think, *If only my son would work harder in school, leave those immature friends behind, etc. If only my daughter would act kinder, be more honest, etc.* St. Katharine Drexel found herself challenged to do what she thought others should do. If you hold your tongue and take your advice to become a better role model, how will this affect your child's behavior?

10. Humility is hardly a popular concept. Can you recall the last time you talked about it, or even used the word in a conversation? (Reading the Beatitudes in church doesn't count.) Can you remember an example when you complimented someone on their humility? How can we work toward a state in which

the idea is so basic and rewarding that we consider it a part of everyday life? How can we change our reality?

Appendix:
Prayers of the Rosary

The Sign of the Cross

In the name of the Father, and of the Son, and of the Holy Spirit. Amen.

Apostles' Creed

I believe in God, the Father almighty, creator of heaven and earth. I believe in Jesus Christ, his only Son, our Lord. He was conceived by the power of the Holy Spirit and born of the Virgin Mary. He suffered under Pontius Pilate, was crucified, died, and was buried. He descended to the dead. On the third day he rose again. He ascended into heaven, and is seated at the right hand of the Father. He will come again to judge the living and the dead. I believe in the Holy Spirit, the holy catholic Church, the communion of saints, the forgiveness of sins, the resurrection of the body, and the life everlasting. Amen.

Our Father

Our Father, who art in heaven, hallowed be thy name; thy kingdom come; thy will be done on earth as it is in heaven. Give us this day our daily bread; and forgive us our trespasses as we forgive those who trespass against us; and lead us not into temptation, but deliver us from evil. Amen.

Glory Be to the Father

Glory to the Father, and to the Son, and to the Holy Spirit: as it was in the beginning, is now, and will be forever. Amen.

Hail Mary

Hail Mary, full of grace, the Lord is with you. Blessed are you among women, and blessed is the fruit of your womb, Jesus. Holy Mary, Mother of God, pray for us sinners, now and at the hour of our death. Amen.

Hail, Holy Queen

Hail, holy Queen, Mother of mercy,
hail, our life, our sweetness, and our hope.
To you we cry, the children of Eve;
to you we send up our sighs,
mourning and weeping in this land of exile.
Turn, then, most gracious advocate,
your eyes of mercy toward us;
lead us home at last
and show us the blessed fruit of your womb, Jesus:
O clement, O loving, O sweet Virgin Mary.
Amen.

Resources

Ahern, Patrick. *Maurice and Thérèse: The Story of a Love.* New York: Doubleday, 1998.

Anonymous. *Go Ask Alice.* New York: Aladdin Paperbacks, 1998.

Artress, Lauren. *Walking a Sacred Path: Rediscovering the Labyrinth as a Spiritual Tool.* New York: Riverhead Books, 1995.

St. Augustine. *The Confessions.* Translated by Maria Boulding, O.S.B. Vintage Spiritual Classics. New York: Vintage Books, 1997.

Bernard-Marie, O.F.S., and Jean Huscenot, F.E.C. *Conversations of the Saints: Words of Wisdom from God's Chosen.* Translated by Victoria Hébert and Denis Sabourin. Liguori, MO: Liguori Publications, 1999.

Buchholz, Ester Schaler. *The Call of Solitude: Alonetime in a World of Attachment.* Simon and Schuster, 1999.

Calamari, Barbara, and Sandra DiPasqua. *Novena: The Power of Prayer.* New York: Penguin Studio, 1999.

Cousineau, Phil. *The Art of Pilgrimage: The Seeker's Guide to Making Travel Sacred.* Berkeley, CA: Conari Press, 1998.

Cowan, Tom. *The Way of the Saints: Prayers, Practices, and Meditations.* New York: Perigee, 2000.

Cristiani, Léon. *Saint Monica and Her Son Augustine.* Translated by M. Angeline Bouchard. 2d ed. Boston: St. Paul Books and Media, 1994.

Donofrio, Beverly. *Looking for Mary, or The Blessed Mother and Me.* New York: Viking Compass, 2000.

Dubruiel, Michael, comp. *Mention Your Request Here: The Church's Most Powerful Novenas*. Huntington, IN: Our Sunday Visitor, 2000.

Dues, Greg. *Catholic Customs and Traditions: A Popular Guide*. Rev. ed. Mystic, CT: Twenty-Third Publications, 2000.

Giannetti, Charlene C. *Who Am I? . . . And Other Questions of Adopted Kids*. New York: Price Stern Sloan, 1999.

Giannetti, Charlene C., and Margaret Sagarese. *Parenting 911: How to Safeguard and Rescue Your 10- to 15-Year-Old from Substance Abuse, Depression, Sexual Encounters, Violence, Failure in School, Danger on the Internet, and Other Risky Situations*. New York: Broadway Books, 1999.

———. *The Roller-Coaster Years: Raising Your Child through the Maddening Yet Magical Middle School Years*. New York: Broadway Books, 1997.

Kelly, Sean, and Rosemary Rogers. *Saints Preserve Us!: Everything You Need to Know about Every Saint You'll Ever Need*. New York: Random House, 1993.

Lang, J. Stephen. *1,001 Things You Always Wanted to Know about the Bible (But Never Thought to Ask)*. Nashville, TN: Thomas Nelson, 1999.

La Plante, Alice, and Clare La Plante. *Heaven Help Us: The Worrier's Guide to the Patron Saints*. New York: Dell, 1999.

Lovasik, Lawrence G. *Treasury of Novenas*. New York: Catholic Book Publishing Company, 1986.

Maguire, C. E. *Saint Madeleine Sophie Barat*. New York: Sheed and Ward, 1960.

The New American Bible. New York: Catholic Book Publishing Company, 1990.

The New Jerusalem Bible. New York: Doubleday, 1998.

One Hundred Saints. Boston: Little, Brown and Company, 1993.

Strathern, Paul. *St. Augustine in 90 Minutes*. Chicago: Ivan R. Dee, 1997.

St. Thérèse of Lisieux. *Story of a Soul: The Autobiography of Saint Thérèse of Lisieux*. Translated by John Clarke, O.C.D. 3d ed. Washington, DC: ICS Publications, 1996.

West, Melissa Gayle. *Exploring the Labyrinth: A Guide for Healing and Spiritual Growth*. New York: Broadway Books, 2000.

Wilkes, Paul. *Beyond the Walls: Monastic Wisdom for Everyday Life*. New York: Doubleday, 1999.